A Pictorial History

Lubbock

The backbones of the early economy around Lubbock; cattle and cotton. This may have represented the entire local cotton crop in 1897.

Because it provided scarce water, the windmill was vital to the growth of Lubbock. In the background is the first county courthouse, completed in 1892. Courtesy of The Museum, Texas Tech University

Lubbock

A Pictorial History

Nancy Brooker Bronwell

Design by Jamie Backus

The Donning Company/Publishers
Virginia Beach, Virginia

Five dudes! Obviously, they want to "make assurance doubly sure." Everybody is packing a pistol and a rifle. The belts are strictly functional to fighting, since all men are wearing suspenders.

Photographed about 1910, when posses were not uncommon, these men seem to be taking a brief respite from pursuit of either animals or desperados. According to Justice of the Peace dockets, about 1907, early Lubbock residents were astonishingly rowdy at times. Several murders occurred during the early 1900s. One early sheriff pursuing a thief into the open countryside, both on horseback, reached a point about ten miles out of town. At full gallop, he drew his pistol, took aim, and proceeded to shoot his own horse through the head. He walked home. Courtesy of The Museum, Texas Tech University

For information write: The Donning Company/Publishers, 5041 Admiral Wright Road, Virginia Beach, Virginia 23462.

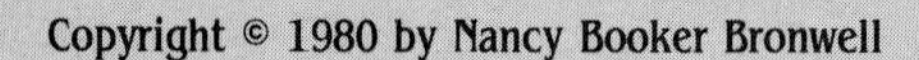

Library of Congress Cataloging in Publication Data:

Bronwell, Nancy.
Lubbock, a pictorial history.

Includes index.
1. Lubbock, Tex.—Description—View. 2. Lubbock, Tex.—History—Pictorial works. I. Title.

F394.L9B76 976.4'847 80-22748
ISBN 0-89865-076-3

Printed in the United States of America

Contents

Lubbock square, from the top of the courthouse, about the middle 1920s. Sidewalks had been added, and the trees, planted some years before, were thriving despite the lack of moisture. Look at all the Model Ts! The town was becoming prosperous. Courtesy of Southwest Collection, Texas Tech University

Foreword

During the forty-four years I served as Lubbock's Representative in the United States Congress, 1934-1978, I had a unique and unbroken view of Lubbock, of its constantly amazing growth and development. While I made countless personal visits to Lubbock and environs throughout those years, the vantage point I had from Washington, 2,000 miles removed, enabled me to "see the fire unobscured by the smoke."

The essential ingredient of our growth and progress has been the quality of our people and our institutions. Drought, hail, the tornado, and other ills have not defeated us. Nancy Bronwell's *Lubbock: A Pictorial History* reflects in both pictures and words the indomitable spirit of the people of Lubbock and their heritage.

I am not a prophet, but I do not hesitate to predict a bright future for Lubbock and the Lubbock area. The beat is—and doubtless will continue to be—up!

—George H. Mahon
Lubbock, Texas

A chuckwagon on the Matador Ranch in 1885. This view shows the cook's supply end of the wagon. The cook, a vital man on the trail drive, always carried sourdough starter for biscuits, and one old rancher recently remarked, "The best peach cobbler I ever put in my mouth was off the back of a chuckwagon." These men are working cowboys—nary a Gary Cooper in the bunch—and they're hungry. Courtesy of Southwest Collection, Texas Tech University

Preface

The Lubbock Symphony Orchestra in 1978, William A. Harrod conducting. Harrod has been the conductor since the orchestra began in 1946. Twenty-six musicians showed up for the first rehearsal, many of whom had returned to the city after serving during World War II at Lubbock Army Air Base (Graves, History of Lubbock*).*

Former dean of students James. G. Allen, now director of the Texas Tech Dads' Association, who has been closely associated with the symphony over the years, says, "My ultimate conviction is that the symphony has been the truest bellwether and litmus paper for cultural advancement in Lubbock. The symphony was originally the projection of some adopted sons of West Texas who fell in love with the community while they were at the Lubbock Army Air Base. They furnished the initial leadership and insisted on staying with it. Initially, the bowing of the home talents' violins may have left something to be desired, but the spirit was there." And that spirit remains. Artists and conductors from all over the nation perform with the symphony and offer praise for its spirit and talent. Courtesy of Dean James G. Allen, photo Courtesy of Lubbock Symphony

This book is dedicated to Lubbock's friends and neighbors, known and unknown—to those past, present, and future whose indomitable spirit and courage have helped to weave the fabric of a community into a tapestry of survival, strength, and excellence in the face of overwhelming odds.

Lubbock: A Pictorial History was written in the spirit conveyed by the words of Will and Ariel Durant: "The heritage that we can now . . . transmit is richer than ever before. . . . To those of us who study history not merely as a warning reminder of man's follies and crimes, but also as an encouraging remembrance of generative souls, the past . . . becomes a celestial city. . . ."

To thank adequately all my friends and neighbors who shared their pictures and reminiscences would require another volume. My deep thanks go to them and to Etta Lynch; to Dr. David Murrah and Janet Neugebauer of the Southwest Collection, Texas Tech University; to Dr. Leslie Drew and his staff, The Museum, Texas Tech University, particularly Betty Mills and Rosie Montgomery; to the Ranching Heritage Headquarters, Texas Tech University; to Dr. Lauro Cavazos, president of Texas Tech University and Medical School and the Texas Tech Health Sciences Center; to Professor Reed Quilliam, Texas Tech University Law School; and to Bea Zeeck and the Texas Tech University Public Information Office. Additional thanks go to Robert Norris, publisher, Jay Harris, editor, the *Avalanche-Journal;* to the Lubbock Chamber of Commerce, John Logan and his staff; to the staff of the George and Helen Mahon Library; to Reese Air Force Base; and to Bill Griggs' group.

My thanks also to my unofficial archivist, Dorothy Rylander; to Evelyn Gaffga; and to Frances Harris.

Finally, but not least, my thanks to Dr. Lawrence Graves and his associates, without whom nothing would have been written about Lubbock.

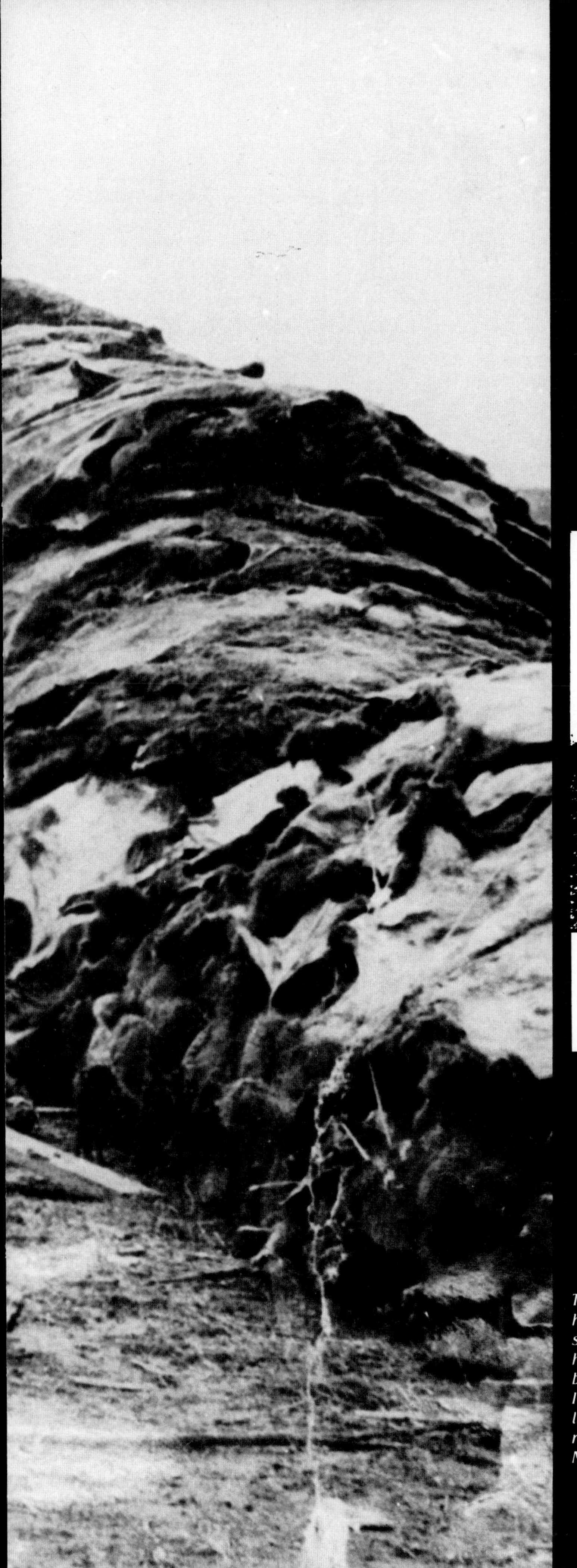

Chapter 1

1878-1900

This pile of buffalo hides only hints at the enormity of the slaughter of the Plains buffalo herds from 1870 until they became extinct. When the Indians lost the buffalo, their livelihood, they were forced onto reservations. Courtesy of The Museum, Texas Tech University

In the background of this typical Comanche nomad camp, a woman processes a buffalo hide. In the foreground, a woman packs a travois, the horse-drawn sled which moved the tribe's belongings. Courtesy of Lubbock Chamber of Commerce

Chief Quanah Parker some time after he entered the reservation in Oklahoma in 1875. Captured by Comanches at the age of nine, in 1836, his mother married Chief Peta Nocona when she was eighteen. Quanah was born in 1845 at Cedar Lake, near what is now Seminole, Texas, about ninety miles southwest of Lubbock. His mother named him "Quanah"— "Fragrant"—after the spring flowers. He died on the reservation in Oklahoma in February 1911 and in 1957 was reinterred with full military honors at Fort Sill. His six remaining children attended. His mother died in 1864 while living with her brother. She had been returned to her family three years earlier but continued to pine for her Indian way of life on the Staked Plains.

After, but not because of, an encounter with Ranald Mackenzie, Quanah led his people onto the reservation in 1875. This opened up the area for white settlers. Charles Goodnight established his ranch on the Plains in 1876.

At one point, a federal official suggested that Quanah become a Christian and live like one. "Go home," he advised, "and tell your wives that all but one must leave."

He considered this, briefly. "You go tell 'em which one I keep." He remained polygamous. Picture from Western History Collections, University of Oklahoma, Norman, Oklahoma

In early 1878, on a desolate stretch of the South Plains of Texas, a group of men squatted around a dying campfire, occasionally tossing handfuls of buffalo chips into the flame. Weary but satisfied, twenty-nine-year-old Paris Cox leaned back against the spokes of the wagon wheel and chewed a green grass stem. He'd made up his mind. This was going to be his land.

He peered into the darkness, hearing the rustle of the tall, dried grasses, savoring the rich prairie smells coming in on the rising, incessant wind. He heard a coyote's eerie howl in the distance. As the wagon wheel sank a bit into the sandy soil, Cox shifted his weight. The wagon was loaded with buffalo hides and bones, the results of the latest hunt. Considering that buffalo hunters had wiped out the last of the large herds in 1877, he'd had wonderful luck and the hides should bring a good price.

Four years before, in 1875, he had traded his thriving Indiana sawmill and lumber company for 5,000 acres of public domain land in Texas, and the deal was already looking better than he had anticipated. Since he'd never seen the land, he'd taken a real gamble when the Texas railroad agent had offered him the exchange. Cox and his wife, Mary Ferguson, had married when he moved from North Carolina to Indiana, and they both shared a deep Quaker trust in the beneficence of the Almighty.

But Cox believed in doing everything he could to get it on his own.

Until the hunt, he'd never seen any land formation like the Caprock. As the men had approached the hunting grounds, Cox had marveled at the looming escarpment that stretched across the arid landscape. Resembling a gigantic table, the Caprock rose abruptly more than 1,000 feet above the surrounding West Texas plain.

Ten million years before, heavy rains had run off the mountains to the west, and modified by wind, rain and frost, had gradually brought about formation of a mesa-like table land, forming the High Plains, or as the Spanish explorers had called it, the Llano Estacado—the Staked Plain. Water rose to the surface, evaporated and deposited calcium to form a hard layer of caliche twelve inches to fourteen inches below the surface. At deeper levels, water formed a reserve that resulted in rich topsoil and plentiful grassland, as well as drinking water from wells.

Between buffalo hunts, Cox spent long hours examining this new land. At one point, he discovered a canyon, the filled remains of an ancient deep river bed. When he found the ashes of old campfires and the bones of small animals, and saw several small lakes, he realized that this sheltered location had been a camping site for nomadic Apache and Comanche Indians who once roamed the Plains. Once, he found an arrowhead. Occasionally, he spotted an Indian riding alone, but none ever made any effort to approach him.

Because of its texture, the soil retained much of the scarce rainfall. This produced lush grass, and after a good rain, hundreds of playa lakes dotted the area. The ambitious Cox reasoned that a land which could grow such verdant grass could grow other, more profitable crops. As the records show, at least one settler, Hank Smith, had recently established a ranching operation in the area, and his cattle were prospering. So Cox made the arduous 450-mile trip to Austin, filed for title to the West Texas land, arranged for surveying, and returned to the Plains. Smith agreed to dig him a well and plant twenty-three acres of crops. With his seed grain in the ground, he climbed into his wagon and set out for Indiana to bring his family to Texas.

In October 1879, the Cox family neared their new homestead, accompanied by three other Quaker families, the Stubbs, Spray, and Hayworth families. As the wagons approached the Caprock and the straining horses inched up the steep slope through a gap in the forbidding rock, only Paris Cox knew what awaited them at the top. After reaching the summit, he rested the horses while the newcomers stared open-mouthed at the flat grassland that stretched endlessly in every direction. The horizon seemed even to turn upward, extending vision to infinity. The new arrivals were accustomed to green Indiana vegetation which turned to russet and gold in the fall. Here, no trees and only a few scrub bushes relieved the monotony of the desolate table-like land. A hawk wheeled lazily overhead in the cloudless blue sky, searching for one of the swift, big-eared jackrabbits or small brown prairie dogs scurrying for shelter in one of the thousands of holes dotting the landscape. These holes posed a real threat to livestock, which often stumbled into one, broke a leg, and had to be destroyed.

When the travelers finally arrived at their destination, they and their animals were exhausted from the long journey. But the first urgent order of business was shelter. Wood was scarce, but Cox had foresightedly picked up some stout branches along creek beds below the Caprock. He split the timbers and began digging earth and roots for sod bricks to build a house. He cut them into two-foot-long blocks, then placed them in pairs lengthwise, then in pairs crosswise, like bricks. This formed a solid wall two feet thick to withstand both heat and cold. Braced by timbers, sod was laid for the roof. Cox could have built the type of shelter itinerant sheepmen and cattlemen had originated—a full- or half-dugout. They dug these shelters four or five feet below ground level, usually facing southeast or south to avoid cold winds or, in summer, to invite a cooling breeze. After they erected sod walls of equal height, and sod roofs, they would hang cattle hides to cover the walk-in door. The other Quaker families pitched tents. They named their settlement Estacado.

That year, 1879, the settlers gathered an abundant harvest while enjoying warm days and cool nights. But November brought an abrupt change. One day, within moments, the atmosphere became deathly still. No blade of grass stirred. The animals began to low and whinny, stirring restlessly. Within a half-hour, an ominous reddish-gray front loomed on the horizon to the north, and a howling sand storm descended on the miserable little band. Vicious, killer winds, loaded with gritty particles of sand, swept in inexorably from the north, howling with banshee wails. They keened through gaps in the flimsy canvas tents, beating the frail dwellings to shredded ribbons. Relatively secure in their sod house, the Coxes despaired to see their neighbors' tents demolished, but did what they could to help. This community spirit has become the hallmark of life on the South Plains.

Not only did the elements attack the settlers: Deadly rattlesnakes which abounded on the plains often slithered into the dwellings; scorpions and tarantulas made themselves at home. One morning, Mrs. Hayworth found a gigantic, furry spider in her milk pail. Wolves and even cowardly coyotes ventured close to the settlement to eat the entrails from slaughtered game. Their howls drove the women almost to hysteria.

By spring of 1880, all but the Cox family had decided they couldn't cope with such terrible anguish and adversity. So the disgruntled pioneers loaded their meager possessions into the wagons and fled back to safety in Indiana. Unfortunately, they left before they had had time to experience a unique South Plains phenomenon: the tranquil, clear days that can follow bitter sandstorms and which endear the Plains to its inhabitants.

Nevertheless, Paris and Mary Cox, their family, and one hired man, George Corskadon, remained, and in June 1880, Mary gave birth to Bertha Cox. An old Quaker friend, Dr. William Hunt, arrived from his station in Osage Indian Territory to officiate at Bertha's arrival. In turn, Dr. Hunt brought his own family to Estacado on June 15, 1881. The 1880 census shows only the Coxes and Corskadon living in the county.

In the same year in which Bertha was born, one George Singer came into the area and built a store at the northwest end of the long canyon Cox had discovered in 1878 (later to be named Yellowhouse Canyon from two yellow houses there). The store was next to one of several of the canyon lakes which were supplied by springs. In addition to being a general store, it served as a post office, way station for travelers, and gathering place for Mexicans, cowboys, and the settlers who were soon straggling into the country. Today, the site is marked with a historical marker. Of course, all supplies had to be freighted in by wagons from towns miles to the east—Denison, Sherman and Fort Worth.

In the spring of 1890, W. E. Rayner, part-owner of the Rayner Cattle Company who ranched in King County, came to the South Plains. W. D. Crump, another settler, had been interested in establishing a town called Monterey. Frank Wheelock and some of his friends also became interested in the operation and eventually banded together to establish the town of Lubbock on the north side of Yellowhouse Canyon. After some discussion, on December 19, 1890, the two rival groups, Wheelock and Rayner, agreed to consolidate the two towns and move them to the present site of Lubbock (Graves, *History of Lubbock*).

While the Quakers struggled to tame the raw Texas land, another significant development was taking place. Speculators in England and Scotland, hearing profit knocking, began to form syndicates to invest in purchases of large tracts of land offered by the railroads. Long connoisseurs of fine cattle, the syndicates bought large parcels of rich grass land for twenty-five to fifty cents per acre. Three or four years later, they sold the land, tripling and sometimes quadrupling their profits. American speculators quickly became intrigued and lost little time in the rush to join in the profiteering.

In 1884, in Davenport, Iowa, J. S. Keator, William O. Kulp, Stillman Wheelock, and others formed the Western Land Live Stock Company. It capitalized for $800,000 and started operations in Texas; its first headquarters were at Fort Worth. The company's brand was IOA, but this lent itself to such easy alteration into many other brands that the IOA Ranch soon lost hundreds of cattle to enterprising thieves.

Starting in June 1885, a series of disasters hit the IOA operation. A terrible drought lasted into the fall of 1887, decimating the herds. To make matters worse, during an especially severe blizzard that winter, the cattle, driven to a fence, broke it down, and much of the herd drifted hundreds of miles to the south and were never recovered. In addition, the price of cattle went from twenty-five dollars a head in 1885 to five dollars a head or less in 1887. Another drawback to successful cattle raising was the presence of wild mustang herds, which often lured domestic cattle away from the range.

By 1891, most of the capital investment of the IOA had disappeared. Another drought, lasting three years, came along in 1891 and ruined the IOA. Their few remaining assets were foreclosed and sold November 1901. In effect, this freed land for development into smaller parcels.

During the latter half of 1890, a wave of farmers came into the Lubbock area to settle permanently. They established a local government in country which had already, by the Texas Constitution of 1876, divided the West Texas area into county units. The merger of the Wheelock and the Rayner groups in 1890 spared the area a fight for the county seat (Graves, *History of Lubbock*).

Lubbock was on its way to becoming an organized town.

About 1878, Paris Cox and his family saw the same Caprock as do today's travellers. Shown from above Post, Texas, thirty-five miles south of Lubbock, the ancient escarpment rises to the Llano Estacado, or Staked Plains, which stretch far to the north. From Ed Neff, Post, Texas

General Nelson A.Miles, (1839-1925), began his military career as a young lieutenant of volunteers during the Civil War. At age seventeen, after the war ended, he decided on a military career. He had become a major-general despite the lack of a West Point background, which, at that time, was considered necessary to promotion. He was then routinely commissioned as a colonel. In 1874, he came from the North to the Staked Plains of Texas, assigned to stop the depredations of the Kiowas and Comanches. When the winter was over, Miles had driven Sitting Bull into Canada and rendered Chief Crazy Horse impotent to continue his operations; he also succeeded in finally capturing Chief Joseph of the Nez Perces, opening up the Plains to permanent settlers who heretofore had not dared bring their families to live in a territory populated by savages and eventually making the city of Lubbock possible. The last Indian was seen around the courthouse square about 1901.

This picture was probably taken shortly before Miles retired in Washington on August 8, 1903. The wooden structure behind him is typical of army posts. The Congressional Medal of Honor hangs about his collar. From Johnson, The Unregimented General; *courtesy of The Museum, Texas Tech University*

General Ranald S. Mackenzie, (1840-1888), was famous for his bloody encounters with Indians and his success in driving them from the South Plains area, clearing the way for permanent settlers. Mackenzie was a West Pointer who had met Miles during the Civil War when Mackenzie commanded a cavalry detachment under General Sherman. While Miles was fighting on the Staked Plains, Mackenzie was receiving recognition for his capture of the hostile Indian village in Palo Duro canyon in September, 1874. His lengendary temper was ascribed to a blow on the head. Eventually, he became unable to function, and had to be confined to an asylum in New York, where he died. From Johnson, The Unregimented General; *courtesy of The Museum, Texas Tech University*

Harvey Underhill, father of Rachel Underhill (Mrs. George W. Singer) and Lina Underhill (Mrs. Joseph Sherman), lived at Estacado in the 1880s. Courtesy of The Museum, Texas Tech University

In October 1879, this intrepid pioneer, Paris Cox, arrived with his family from Indiana in a covered wagon with all their household goods. He founded the town of Estacado, which later joined with W. E. Rayner's "Ray Town" on the opposite side of the Yellowhouse Canyon and moved to a third site north of what is now Lubbock, at the site of the present Lubbock Country Club. Courtesy of The Museum, Texas Tech University

During the dreadful winter of 1879-80, the first Quaker families, living in tents, endured many of these devastating storms, which drove all but the Cox family back to Indiana. Courtesy of Southwest Collection, Texas Tech University

Rachel Underhill at age fourteen in 1869, holding her Bible. Her dress, typical of a child of that period (and at that time a fourteen-year-old was still considered a child— teenagers were unknown), is undoubtedly homemade and probably of calico.

She and her husband, George W. Singer, founded the first store in Lubbock, Singer's Store, in the Yellowhouse Canyon, a few miles northwest of Lubbock (Graves, History of Lubbock*). It was the post office, saloon, grocery store, and general gathering place for cowboys, and, according to Rollie Burns, "a motley crowd of cowboys, a few Mexicans, and a half-dozen Apache Indians." Courtesy of The Museum, Texas Tech University*

Will Singer, George Singer's father, just after the Civil War. Courtesy of Southwest Collection, Texas Tech University

In 1880, George Singer established his store northeast of Lubbock. It is now located only by a marker. Courtesy of Southwest Collection, Texas Tech University

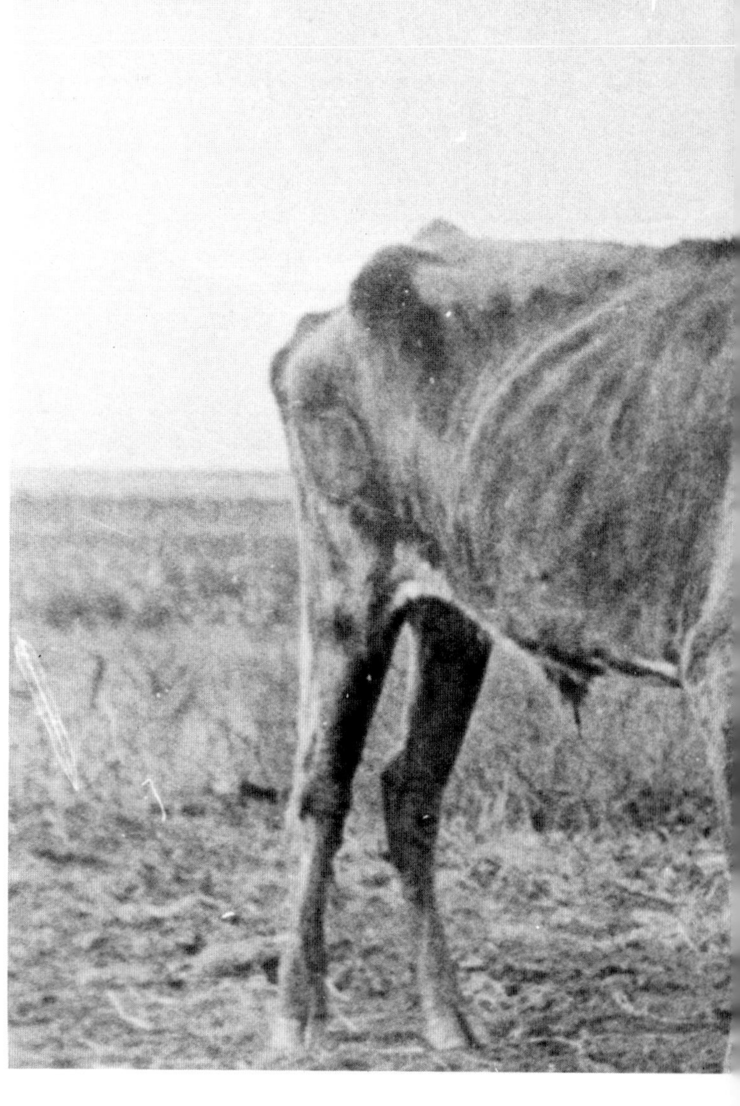

Henry Cannon, who had been a soldier in the Civil War and came West for his health. Will Singer helped him, but Cannon died of tuberculosis. Courtesy of The Museum, Texas Tech University

The epitome of the South Plains: a longhorn steer, probably shown about March, after a hard winter on the range. He is one of the last of his breed. Shortly after 1889, according to Graves (History of Lubbock), most ranchers shifted to Hereford (whiteface) cattle in order to improve their herds. Courtesy of The Museum, Texas Tech University

Victor Culp, prior to 1890, is dressed in the clothing cowboys wore around town during the winter while waiting for ranch work to start in the spring. Courtesy of The Museum, Texas Tech University

In 1933, a Lubbock group dedicated a marker on the site of George Singer's store, which had been demolished years before. Among those attending were: H. Bailey Carroll, second from left, with hand on his waist; Dr. William Curry Holden, sixth from left, holding white hat; Rollie Burns, tenth from left, holding white hat; Liff Sanders, twelfth from left, with beard; Elizabeth West, eighth from right, dressed in black. The others are unidentified. Courtesy of Southwest Collection, Texas Tech University

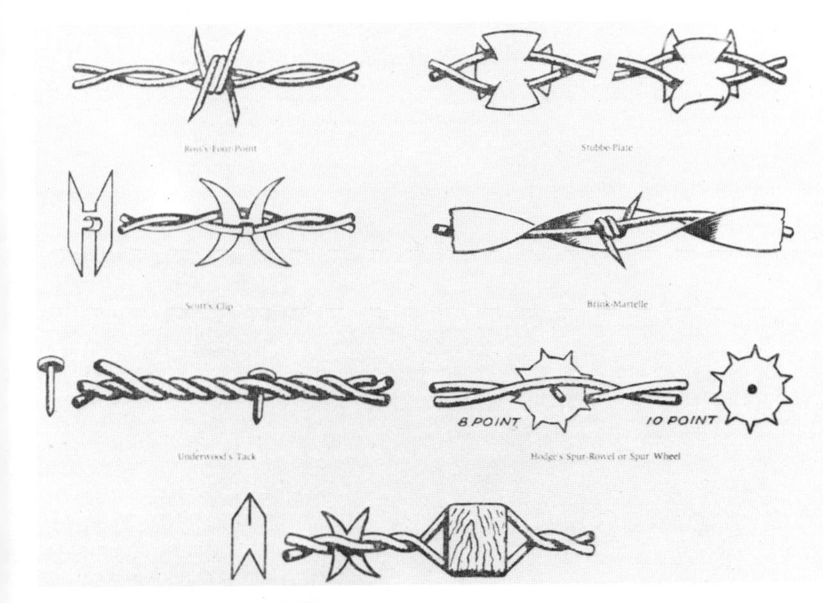

Barbed wire signified the end of the open range and the long cattle drives. Here are some samples among more than 100 different styles. By 1880, the large ranchers had fenced most of the land below the Caprock, and only the smaller herds occupied the Lubbock area. Drawings by Ben Carlton Mead; courtesy Southwest Collection, Texas Tech University

During the long, dreary winters on the ranches, cowboys performed chores in deep snow, stinging blizzards, and choking dust. With limited resources at hand, cowboys had to create their own entertainment. Because few female dancing partners were available, some Slaughter Lazy S cowboys are engaging in a "stag" dance, accompanied by a fiddle. Custom dictated that each man take several turns being what they termed "heifer-branded": The cowboy either wore an apron or tied a handkerchief about his arm to designate that he was taking the female partner's turn.

Occasionally, on the Fourth of July or Christmas, the ranch owner and his wife would arrange a dinner or large dance and bring in real women. People arrived from miles around, and dancing continued for several days, always until daybreak. Tables were set with ham, turkeys, and assorted pies. Children slept in the wagons, or in inclement weather, in the back room on pallets. Courtesy of Southwest Collection, Texas Tech University

Buffalo on the Goodnight Ranch, about 1887. In 1865, with Oliver Loving, Charles Goodnight drove a herd of cattle from Young County to Fort Sumner, New Mexico (Graves, History of Lubbock*). Later, he established one of the great ranches in the Panhandle. By the time this picture was taken, the last of the herds of the great beasts had thundered through the Plains for the last time. This herd remained under Colonel Goodnight's protection. Courtesy of The Museum, Texas Tech University; photo by Higginbotham Brothers*

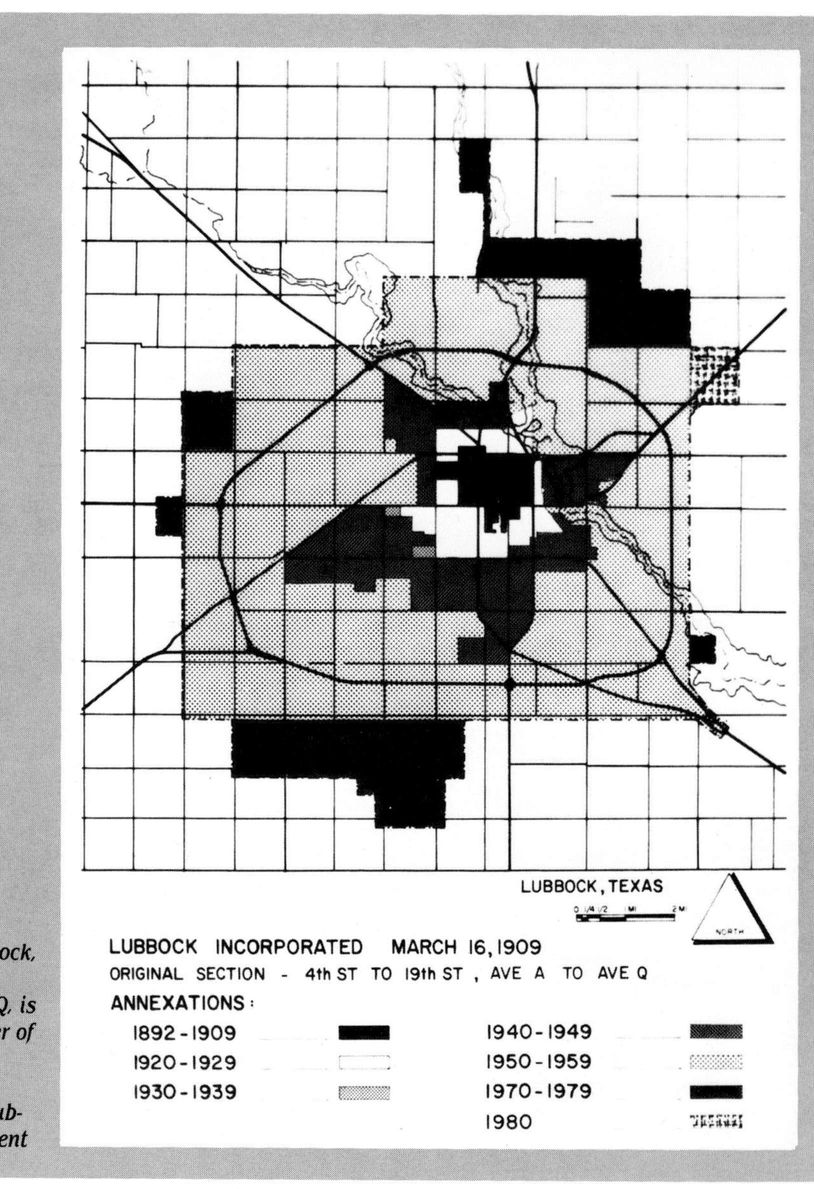

The original section of Lubbock, Fourth Street to Nineteenth Street, Avenue B to Avenue Q, is the dark square in the center of this map which shows the expansion of the city over a seventy-year period. From Lubbock City Planning Department

A Baptist baptism in 1885 in Lubbock County. Baptists were intent on baptism by immersion, and stock tanks, varying in depth from three feet to eighteen feet, were used. The minister and the candidate for baptism are at left, center. The sun forced women and children, dressed in their Sunday best, to wear hats or bonnets. Courtesy of Southwest Collection, Texas Tech University

Taken about 1889, this picture shows one of the earliest homes in Lubbock—the half-dugout. The full-dugout dwellings which preceded this were sunk level with the ground and covered either with scarce lumber topped with sod or with canvas. Stray cattle and drunken cowhands, as well as an occasional, unwary Indian, were known to fall through the roof. Dr. William Hunt, who came to the area in 1879, lived in a full-dugout for a time and has written that while at dinner one night, he was astonished to look up and see a cow's leg crash through the roof.

As primitive as the half-dugout was, it was an improvement over its predecessor; this one has a wooden roof and door. The absence of women may indicate that this was a semi-permanent way station for cowboys on the range. Courtesy of Southwest Collection, Texas Tech University

After the half-dugout and sod houses, the next early Lubbock residences were slat. These simple houses boasted few frills, but they offered much better security from severe elements than earlier dwellings. To the right, a vine grows over a window, forming a natural shade. Some measure of privacy is afforded by the gate and wire fence, and the beginnings of shade are provided by the small tree at left. The house is raised off the ground. The scarce wood used to build this house has been hauled from long distances in horse-drawn wagons. Courtesy of Southwest Collection, Texas Tech University

Frank E. Wheelock built this grand house for his family in 1899. Homes generally faced south to catch the cooling breezes in the summer and to avoid the howling northers and blizzards in the winter. Courtesy of Southwest Collection, Texas Tech University

Mr. and Mrs. Frank Wheelock, who had the first wedding in Lubbock County, in 1889. Courtesy of Southwest Collection, Texas Tech University

This postcard depicts a social gathering of some kind—a barbecue, dinner on the grounds, or possibly a wedding or baptism. Courtesy of The Museum, Texas Tech University

Antelope, early denizens of the South Plains, furnished good eating for Lubbock residents. Properly prepared, the barbecued meat was considered succulent and mouth-watering. Today, in Lubbock, barbecue remains one of the most popular items on the bill-of-fare. M.A. Wood, with his double-barreled rifle, has brought back the meat for the first barbecue in Lubbock, September 1891. Courtesy of The Museum, Texas Tech University

The first Lubbock County courthouse was completed in 1892 at a cost of approximately $12,000. In April 1895, a severe sandstorm blew in and warped the courthouse so badly that it was actually twisted, and the doors couldn't be closed. The tower was blown off and never replaced. Before the builders could repair the damage, they had to remove the roof entirely (Graves, History of Lubbock*). Courtesy of Lubbock Chamber of Commerce*

By 1888, more Quakers had flocked to Estacado and more children had been born on the Plains. The community was growing rapidly. The simple church architecture is typical not only of the plain Quaker way of life, but also of the newly built wood structures. Wood was hauled by freight wagon from Amarillo and Colorado City. The somber, simple garb reflects the attitude of the Plain People, as they called themselves. Courtesy of Southwest Collection, Texas Tech University; Cory photo by Daniel Studios

Farmers and ranchers needed a central supply depot. About 1890, J. D. Caldwell's store opened for business. Freight wagons hauled lumber, groceries and household supplies into Estacado from Fort Worth, Amarillo, and Colorado City. Courtesy of Southwest Collection, Texas Tech University

A freight wagon train in 1896. This was the only way to move supplies in and out of town. Courtesy of Southwest Collection, Texas Tech University

Yellowhouse Canyon about 1898. It was a dry year. Courtesy of Southwest Collection, Texas Tech University

Miss Emma Hunt, first teacher at Estacado in Lubbock County, in the late 1890s. Notice the passamanterie embroidery on her dress. . .and that magnificent hat. At that time, ladies wore gloves to protect their hands from the fierce sun.

Present-day Hunt descendants say that the gentleman on the left is Dr. William Hunt, her brother. At the request of his Quaker friend, Paris Cox, he moved to Estacado with his family in 1889 from his post on the Osage Indian Reservation in Indian territory and subsequently delivered the first child born in Estacado (Graves, History of Lubbock*). Courtesy of The Museum, Texas Tech University*

Previously located at the site of Estacado, in early 1891 the Nicollet Hotel was moved "intact down the North Canyon and across the Yellowhouse to a site on the square of the new town. Frank Bowles told. . . that some freighters from Colorado City were employed to move the building. Mrs. Frank Wheelock told Miss Perkins that only portions of the hotel were dismantled for the move and that even part of the furniture remained in the rooms.

"Frank Wheelock named it the Nicollet Hotel after a hotel where he stayed in Minneapolis, Minnesota, and George M. Hunt moved over from Estacado to manage it."

In 1900 and 1901, an outbreak of smallpox occurred, serious enough to justify calling it an epidemic, and patrons of the hotel caught it en masse.

"In 1909, Mrs. Mollie D. Abernathy acquired the Nicollet, papered and painted all forty-five of its rooms, put new furniture in the dining room, and hired B. P. Osborne, former manager of the Amarillo Hotel, to run it.

"For a number of years the Nicollet had an annex on the east side of South Singer Street. In May 1909, Van Sanders and a man named Harden acquired this two-story frame building and reopened it as the Clyde Hotel and Cafe."

Early residents of Lubbock had to make their own fun, and many parties were held in the hotel. Many courtships occurred at these, and other parties, and could the old hotel's walls have talked, what tales would have been told! Quotations from Graves, History of Lubbock, *by permission of Dr. Lawrence L. Graves; photograph courtesy of Lubbock Chamber of Commerce*

Mr. and Mrs. Van Sanders, about 1895. She was the former Lizzie Tubbs, Van's second wife. At this time, most ladies carried parasols to protect their skin from the burning sun. Courtesy of Southwest Collection, Texas Tech University

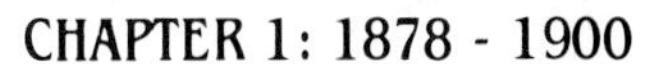

George M. Boles filed for land in Lubbock County, June 17, 1897, and built one of the first big houses. Here he sits on his horse before his handwrought iron fence. Courtesy of Southwest Collection, Texas Tech University

Lubbock's first barbershop moved from Estacado to the new town of Lubbock in 1891. One of these men is Ed T. Cox, the owner. Courtesy of Lubbock Chamber of Commerce

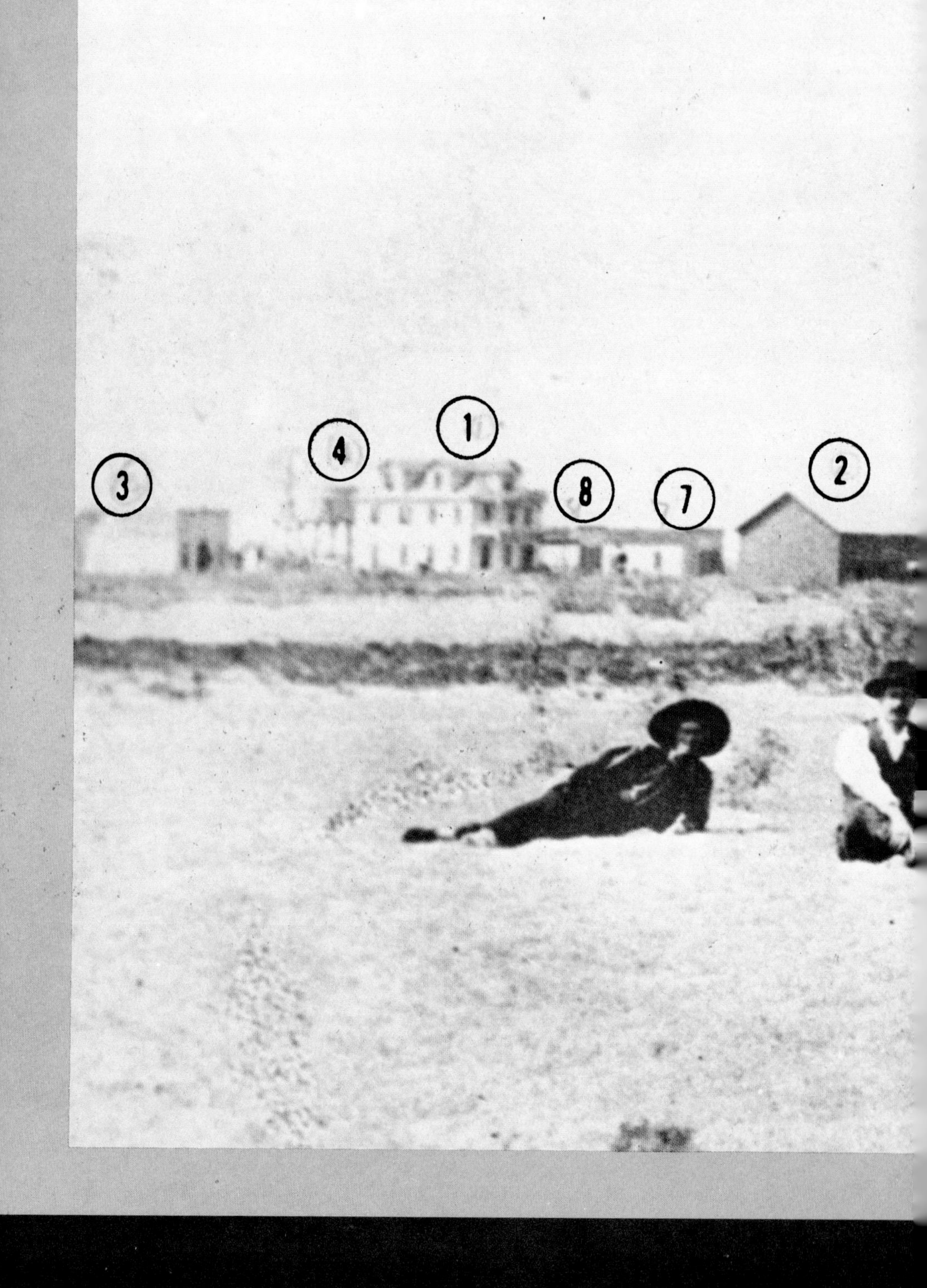

Men on a farm due east of Lubbock, circa 1892. In the background are: (1) Nicollet Hotel, (2) School and jail house, (3) Livery stable, owned by George Wolfforth and Van Sanders, (4) Courthouse under construction, (5) Singer's store, located east of Avenue H at Main Street, (6) J. D. Caldwell's store facing east on Texas Avenue, (7) Blacksmith shop, owned by W. P. Phenix, with barbershop in back, (8) Barbershop; Edward T. Cox, barber, 909 Broadway.

Notice the artistic composition of the men's poses. Each corresponds with almost the exact pose of his opposite number. Courtesy of Southwest Collection, Texas Tech University

6
5

Chapter 2
1900-1920

Yield from the bountiful land at an early Lubbock County Fair, October 8 and 9, 1909. . . a far cry from the Plains of the early settlers, where only tall grass and mesquite grew. Courtesy of Southwest Collection, Texas Tech University

Lubbock grew rapidly during the first decade of the twentieth century. In 1909, Lubbock citizens saw the fruits of their concerted effort to attract the Sante Fe to Lubbock when the first train steamed in. As transportation increased, the population enlarged to 1,938 in Lubbock and 3,624 in Lubbock County, and the economy burgeoned.

About 1903, cotton came to the South Plains. Some argument exists as to who first initiated planting, but by the time the first local gin started operation in 1905, cotton was already an important crop. With the advent of large-scale irrigation in the 1940s, Lubbock was on the road to becoming one of the world's major cotton capitals. More than a half-century later, in 1978, according to the Texas Agricultural Extension Service of the Texas A & M University System, Lubbock and surrounding counties produced 51.1 percent of Texas cotton. What a contrast with the twenty-six bales S. S. Rush harvested in 1901!

Along with the town's economic, agricultural, and commercial growth, Lubbock residents organized cooperative efforts to encourage progress in civic areas. Men's service clubs and women's volunteer and church groups contributed heavily to their neighbors' welfare. Among these cooperative efforts were Trades Days, Cemetery Association, Literary Society, Mothers Club, Lubbock Commercial Club, and the Library Association.

World War I took its toll of the community. Spending for community development slowed; street lighting, transportation, and building suffered for lack of funds. However, the end of the war saw a resurgence in community development.

In early Lubbock, the courthouse square was the center of all commercial activity. In 1906, these farmers have brought their bales to the square to be sold. The first courthouse and windmill are in the background. Courtesy of Lubbock Chamber of Commerce

Lubbock and the South Plains owe an enormous debt of gratitude to Eli Whitney's cotton gin. Nevertheless, while the cotton crop had risen in 1904 to 110 bales from S. S. Rush's half-bale-per acre crop in 1900 and 1902's four bales, all Lubbock cotton had to be ginned at Colorado City.

So, in 1904, Lubbock's community spirit demonstrated itself when people got together and arranged for a gin to be built locally. Since Lubbock had no railroad, the machinery had to be hauled more than 100 miles from Canyon City by wagon.

Cotton production continues to be the backbone of Lubbock's economy. Courtesy of The Museum, Texas Tech University

Alfalfa was a crop in Lubbock County about 1905. Notice the water tank on top of the building in the background. Courtesy of Southwest Collection, Texas Tech University

In the spring of 1901, Baptists started raising funds for a church building. George M. Hunt, a Quaker, gave $100. Eventually, $1,000 was raised, and this building went up on the corner of Avenue G and Thirteenth Street. The Reverend J. R. Miller became the first pastor in 1901.

In the spring of 1915, this structure was moved to a lot on Main Street. The congregation continued to meet at this location until 1946, when the present building was started. Southwestern Bell Telephone Company occupies the old site. Courtesy of Lattimore Ewing

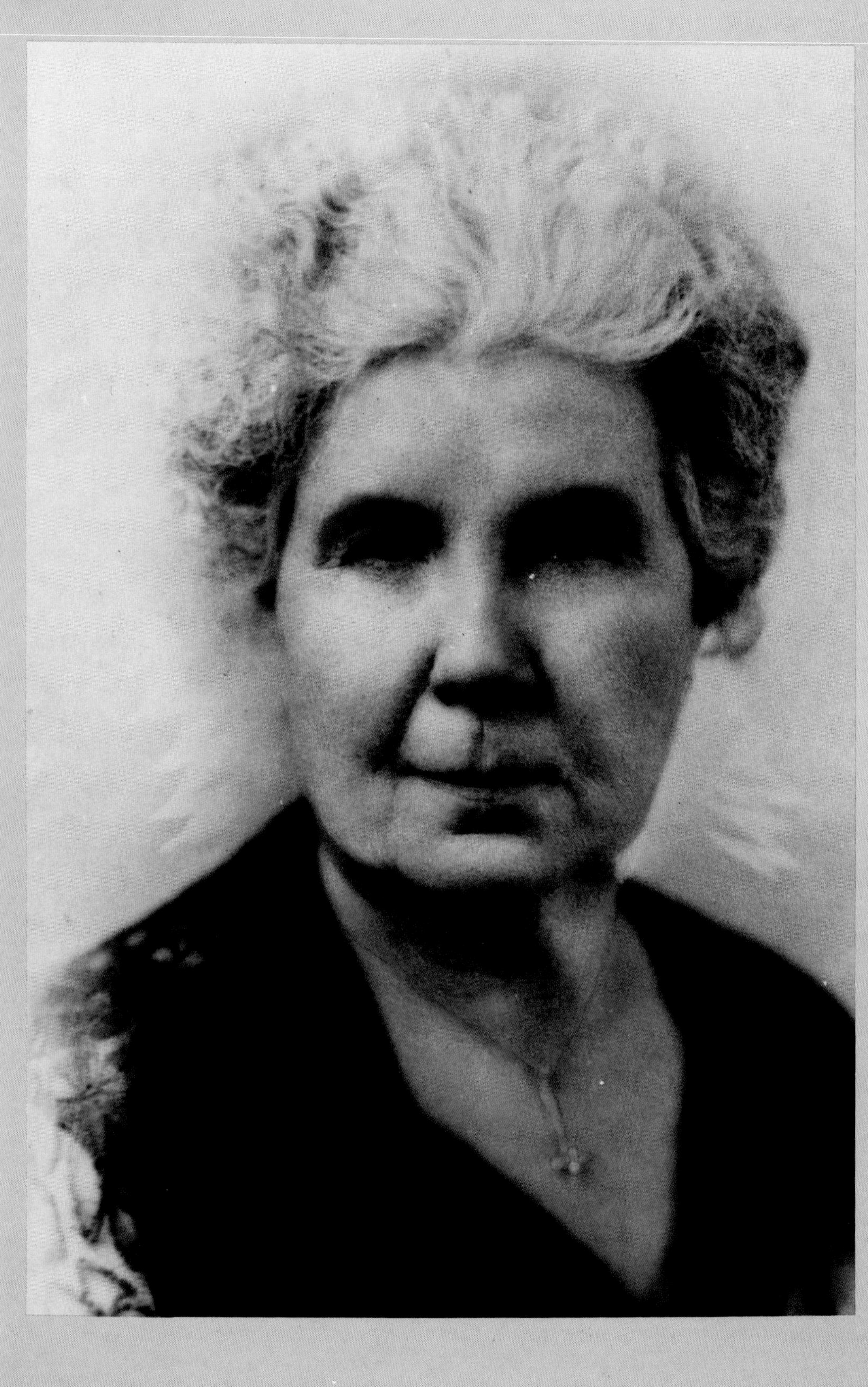

Mollie D. Abernathy, a staunch pioneer whose descendants still live in Lubbock, was born in Hood County, Texas, April 27, 1866. She later married James William Jarrott, who became a member of the Texas State Legislature in 1886, the year of their wedding. Eventually, the family filed on 100 sections of land in West Texas and moved into a tent on the land in 1901. In 1902, a hired gunman assassinated James Jarrott.

*Since Mollie Jarrott had been reared on a ranch, she immediately undertook the family cattle operation. In January 1905, she married Monroe G. Abernathy, a real estate agent. Seymour V. Connor (*Builders of the Southwest*) lists some of her community activities: "She actively engaged in the real estate business, was a charter member of the Lubbock Business and Professional Women's Club. . . interested in women's suffrage, the League of Women Voters and the Women's Christian Temperance Union."*

Her courage and vision helped lay the foundations of the community. Courtesy of Southwest Collection, Texas Tech University

The Lubbock Mercantile Company about 1910 or 1911. The only grocery in town was next door. Courtesy of Lubbock Chamber of Commerce

A Lubbock furniture store—probably the furniture store—in the early 1900s on the courthouse square. The chairs on the mattress at right were used in commerce rather than in homes—for the barbershop, the newspaper office, the mercantile store, and for just generally sittin' and whittlin'. Behind the lad to the left of the group is a rocking cradle, probably made of brass. The firm's delivery wagon is at left foreground. The streets are unpaved. Courtesy of Southwest Collection, Texas Tech University

Walter Posey (1881-1973) was vice-president of the Lubbock Townsite Committee, constituted on May 16, 1906, to induce W. E. Rayner to sell some of his town lots, or to establish a new town. He agreed, and Lubbock was established. In 1909, Posey helped draft the city charter, was a city commissioner, member of the Lubbock Commercial Club, a long-time banker, and civic leader in almost every task undertaken in the community. Dr. Lawrence L. Graves says, "In Lubbock, as Walter Posey once remarked, whenever there was a job to be done everybody pitched in and saw that it got done, whether bringing in a railroad, building a new school, or founding a college." He was an early president of the Lubbock Rotary Club, the first civic club in Lubbock. Courtesy of Lubbock Chamber of Commerce

A 1909 reunion of some of the men who organized Lubbock County in 1891.

Front row, left to right: J. B. Mobley, Irvin L. Hunt, Isham Tubbs, J. J. Reynolds, J. K. Caraway, "Uncle Tang" Martin, Joe Boyd, Joe Boles, J. Andy Wilson, U. G. Moore, and George Boles.

Back row, left to right: Albert Taylor, George C. Wolfforth, Rollie Burns, E. Y. Lee, J. D. Caldwell, Frank Boles, B. O. McWhorter, P. F. Brown, Fred Stubbs, W. A. Carlisle, W. G. Nairn, J. B. Green, Dave Crump, Jerry Burns, Charles Vaughn, Jeff Woods, W. C. Vaughn, Frank Wheelock, C. W. Mallard, J. L. Wilson, and E. B. Green. Courtesy of The Museum, Texas Tech University

Clara Louise Border, now Mrs. Robert Bean of Lubbock, in 1904. She wears a gold ring on her right hand, and her buttoned shoes were fastened with a buttonhook. Some loving hands made that elaborate bonnet. The photographer's bench could not have been comfortable for a small person, and one wonders what thoughts are wandering through that little head to produce such a solemn expression. Courtesy of The Museum, Texas Tech University

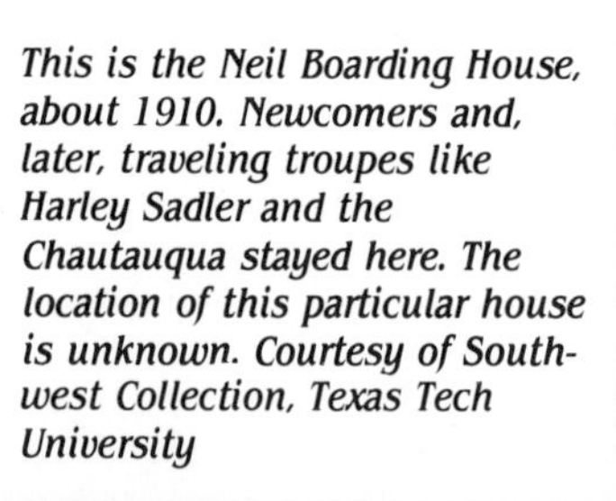

This is the Neil Boarding House, about 1910. Newcomers and, later, traveling troupes like Harley Sadler and the Chautauqua stayed here. The location of this particular house is unknown. Courtesy of Southwest Collection, Texas Tech University

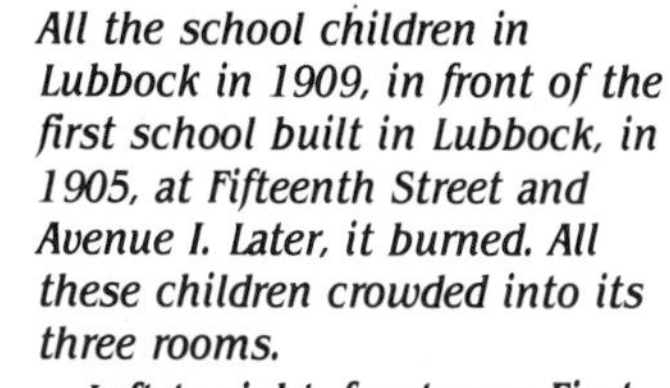

All the school children in Lubbock in 1909, in front of the first school built in Lubbock, in 1905, at Fifteenth Street and Avenue I. Later, it burned. All these children crowded into its three rooms.

Left to right, front row: First three unidentified, Herbert Stubbs, Elwin Wheelock, Emmet Agnew, unidentified, Frank Barclay, Frazier McCrummen, George Reed.

Second row: Hugh Burns, Hoyt Agnew, unidentified, Bob Sanders, Rufus Rush, unidentified, unidentified, Tol Carraway, Clayton McCrummen, Newt Wilson, unidentified, Jim Graves, Earl Sanders, Charlie Graves.

Third row: Winnie Clayton, next four unidentified, Linnie Graves, Pearl Graves, Dovie Green, Minnie Martin, Lillie Barclay, Eva Wheelock, Thelma Carraway, unidentified, Mat Ray, unidentified, Don Clayton, Johnnie Ray, Hattie Sanders, Lucy Tubbs, Carrie Acuff.

Fourth row: Kate Reed, unidentified, Dora Lee, Mary Lee, Fannie Young, unidentified, Courtney Napier, Willie Wilson, unidentified, Thelma (?) Burns, (?) Carraway, Katie Bell Crump, unidentified, Carrie Mae Rush, Tom Clayton, Melissa Elwin (?), unidentified, (?) Clayton, Sid Carraway, John Permey (?).

Fifth row: First two unidentified, Earline Burns, (?) Carraway, Charlie Rush, Max Coleman, unidentified.

Sixth row: Professor Holland, Mrs. Holland, Lula Campbell, Miss Buckley, unidentified.

In the kitchen of the Neil Boarding House, around 1910, the hired girl is cooking at a stove which probably used cow-chips as fuel, due to the scarcity of wood. Courtesy of Southwest Collection, Texas Tech University

A Lubbock area (Acuff) pig-sticking between 1902 and 1908. From left to right: Lilly Quest (Mrs. R. E.) Hoops, R. E. Hoopes, Lennie D. Dalton, Orville Hoopes, Bessie Queen (Mrs. J. W.) Dalton, J. A. Dalton. Courtesy of The Museum, Texas Tech University

One of the first automobiles in Lubbock County, 1907, owned by Rollie Burns. Courtesy of Southwest Collection, Texas Tech University

On the right, Robert Isham Tubbs, who won the first organized rodeo in Lubbock County. On the left is Jennings Winn. Courtesy of Juanelle Windham Tubbs

A Lubbock lumber company before 1909. Courtesy of Southwest Collection, Texas Tech University

Before the coming of the railroad in 1909, wagon trains hauled freight between Lubbock and Amarillo and Lubbock and Colorado City. Here, about 1906, Dr. William G. Hays, hand on hip, stands by his white horse. His son, Robert Wilson Hays, is the small boy on the pony. Mules were used almost exclusively. Dr. David Vigness writes: "In the days before the rails, the responsibility for moving goods fell upon the doughty mule skinners and teamsters who felt lucky if they made the trip from Fort Worth to Lubbock in a month" (in Graves, History of Lubbock*). Courtesy of Southwest Collection, Texas Tech University*

Prior to the coming of the railroad in 1909, merchants hauled all building supplies from Amarillo, Colorado City, or Fort Worth. These drovers have come a long way. Courtesy of Southwest Collection, Texas Tech University

The Hunt family in the early 1900s. Left to right: Irving L. Hunt, Homer Hunt (half-brother to the other three boys), Clifford E. Hunt, George M. Hunt, Allie Hunt. Courtesy of Southwest Collection, Texas Tech University

Old 184—the first railroad train into Lubbock in 1909. Courtesy of Southwest Collection, Texas Tech University

The Santa Fe depot, Lubbock, built in 1910. Courtesy of The Museum, Texas Tech University

At left, C. E. Hunt; at right his brother, A. G. Hunt. C. E. later became administrator at the Lubbock Sanitarium, where he remained until 1953. A. G. (Allie) later owned a grocery store. Two sons live in Lubbock. Allie's son, Homer, is retired, but active in the community. His other son, Dr. Ewell Hunt, together with his partner, Dr. O. W. ("Babe") English, has been in surgical practice since 1934, reportedly the longest-lived surgical partnership in the state of Texas. Their grandfather, George M. Hunt, was the first manager of Frank Wheelock's Nicolett Hotel, owned a store, and was postmaster. Picture courtesy of The Museum, Texas Tech University; legend courtesy of Dr. Ewell Hunt

A parade is always a special event. Here, in 1909, a group of young women on a wagon patriotically wave flags in a Fourth of July gathering and parade at the courthouse square. Courtesy of Lubbock Chamber of Commerce

Miss "Delia" (Adelia) Wilkinson on her horse, about 1910. Her sister married O. L. Slaton, the town banker. The man at left is unidentified. The smart riding habit represents correct attire for ladies, who rode sidesaddle. Courtesy of The Museum, Texas Tech University

Building the trestle to extend the rails for the railroad which arrived in 1909 after several years of desultory paper schemes. Together with the coming of irrigation to the Plains, the coming of the railroad was to become the primary reason for Lubbock's incorporation as a city on March 16, 1909. Courtesy of Lubbock Chamber of Commerce

The Tubbs' old house is still standing and occupied by members of the family. Located about two blocks south of Fourth Street and west of a golf course, it has been maintained in good condition.

In this 1908 picture, stand, left to right: Robert Isham Tubbs; Mrs. J. Lee Tubbs, holding Evelyn Tubbs, who is not yet a year old; J. Lee Tubbs; Travis T. Tubbs; Isham Tubbs, Robert's father; the family cook, Mrs. Gray (they never knew her first name); and Mrs. Isham Tubbs at a distance from the group.

A member of the family reports that Mrs. Isham Tubbs stood so far away because, after the photographer set the poses, Mrs. Gray came rushing out, wiping her hands on her apron, and Mrs. Tubbs refused to stand next to the cook. It seemed to bother Mrs. Gray not at all. Courtesy of Lois Tubbs Patterson

This is a local mercantile company, probably the Lubbock Mercantile Company, in 1910. Look closely and you'll see, at the upper left, a wasp-waisted mannequin. Whether most Lubbock ladies resembled this headless lady is debatable; still, this didn't deter Lubbock housewives from taking advantage of buying the yard goods displayed on the shelves at left and sewing garments for their families. Courtesy of The Museum, Texas Tech University

Max Coleman, at left, behind a chuckwagon, about 1910. Born on January 11, 1888, at Thorp Springs south of Fort Worth, Coleman came with his family to the South Plains in 1889. They camped near the site of the present Lubbock County courthouse. Coleman was graduated from Lubbock High School in 1904. He spent much of his time breaking horses and later ranched with his father. After leaving his ranch about 1918, he wandered through the Northwest. When he returned to Lubbock, having read law for several years, he passed the state bar examination in 1926 (Connor, Builders of the Southwest*).*

In the summer of 1910, Max Coleman, left, and some other cowboys are eating at the Sam Arnett chuckwagon, which camped where Meadow, Texas, is today. Ray Savage is on the ground, eating; he stood guard at night. Jimmy Dunn is the cook. John Rayner and Terrell Allen, for whom the Allen Brothers American Legion Post is named, are riding up. Courtesy of Southwest Collection, Texas Tech University

Mrs. and Mrs. Isham Tubbs in their later years. Courtesy of Lois Tubbs Patterson

Not responsible for goods sent by mail. Not accountable for breakage during transportation.
All claims for errors must be made within Five Days after receipt of goods. After goods are delivered in good order and receipt taken, our responsibility ceases.
Our bills are due here in par funds, and no allowance will be made for exchange or express charges on remittances.

Chicago, 11/28 1902

M Dr. S. H. Windham
Byrds Tex

To **Frank S. Betz & Co.,** Dr.

Manufacturers of All Kinds of
HOT AIR AND VAPOR BATHS, OPERATING TABLES AND CHAIRS, NICKEL PLATERS,
Electrical Apparatus, Surgical Instruments and Appliances, Surgical Dressings,
Compressed Tablets, Supporters, Trusses and Orthopedic Appliances.

Your No.
Our No.
Terms: C.O.D.
Shipped via W.F.X.

SALESROOMS:
35 to 37 Randolph Street

GENERAL OFFICES AND WORKS:
1760-66 E. Ravenswood Park

	1	Watkins Dilator	7 00
	1	Leonard's Dil. Douche	1 00
	1	Elliott's Obstet. Fcp.	3 00
106	1	Tooth Forcep	1 00
13	1	" "	1 00
19	1	" " R.	1 00
19	1	" " L.	1 00
78	1	"	1 00
88	1	" " Root	1 75
2	1	"	1 00
18	1	Graves Vag. Spec.	75
17	1	Hartman's Nasal Spec.	50
	1	Comp. Hix Outfit, Alum Bronze	16 00
90	1	17" Obstet. Bag & Bottles	3 50
24	1	Wild's Forcep	40
77	1	Fixation Eye Fcp., Pl. Straight	70
416	1	Monitor Case	5 50
	1	3" Head Mirror	95
	1	Head Band, With Nose Piece	65
	1	Clayton's Fold Depressor	15
			47 85
		CASH	20 00

27 85

A November 28, 1902, bill from a medical supplies dealer to Dr. Windham. Item #3 on the bill, obstetrical forceps are listed at $3.00. Today, a fourteen-inch obstetrical forceps sells for $78. Courtesy of Juanelle Windham Tubbs

Dr. and Mrs. S. H. Windham of Tahoka, a short distance from Lubbock. Although he practiced medicine in Tahoka, Dr. Windham had many Lubbock interests. This picture was taken shortly after their marriage in 1907.

S. H. Windham was graduated from Sewanee University in Tennessee and Vanderbilt University Medical School. When he came to Tahoka to practice, he met and married Linnie Bigham, the local music teacher. Their daughter, Juanelle (Mrs. Fenner) Tubbs, lives in Lubbock.

The doctor provided well for his family. Mrs. Windham wears a custom-made satin dress. The curtains are lace, and the tablecloth at the extreme right is Battenburg lace, which consisted of strips of material joined with crochet stitches. Mrs. Tubbs has this now.

The statues on the piano are now on the Tubbs mantel in Lubbock. When the little girl's hand broke, Mrs. Windham mended it with surgical gauze and glue. Pianos in affluent homes almost invariably were covered with a scarf of some kind, as here. Courtesy of Juanelle Windham Tubbs

Mrs. George L. Beatty's "Children's Brigade," a literary society, met regularly for several years in Lubbock in the early 1900s.

Front row, left to right: Robert Bean (later a Lubbock judge), Odell Greenhill, F. Benson, Fannie B. Carter, Bernice Wolffarth, Zell Richardson, Katherine May, Martha Caldwell, Fern Wheelock, and Mary Covington.

Back row, left to right: Blanche Bean, Elma Pierce, Ouida Carter, Leila Roberds (Mrs. J. T. Krueger), Opal Ellis, Sally Covington, and Ethel Caldwell.

Several years later, Mrs. Beatty established the Twentieth Century Club. Courtesy of Southwest Collection, Texas Tech University

Early Lubbock brass band, about 1906. Courtesy of Southwest Collection, Texas Tech University

Fishing at Buffalo Springs in the early 1900s. Early Lubbock residents created their own recreation, much of it spent outdoors, so the women wore bonnets, long-sleeved dresses, and gloves to protect their complexions. Today, Buffalo Lakes is a popular fishing spot. Courtesy of Southwest Collection, Texas Tech University

About 1908-1910, several classes of children in the Lubbock Public Schools slicked up, slicked down their cowlicks, were admonished by their mothers, and had their pictures taken. But for the absence of girls, this gathering might have represented the entire population of the Lubbock Public School System at that time. The rug is an excellent example of the kind brought in on earlier freight wagons and later trains for use in South Plains homes.

At far right end, back row, is Wayland Sanders. Courtesy of Southwest Collection, Texas Tech University

Mr. and Mrs. E. A. Teague "slip up" on kids raiding a melon patch, about 1909. Although obviously posed, everybody is joining the fun. Courtesy of The Museum, Texas Tech University

The Temple Ellis family about 1909.

Left to right: Opal Ellis (Mrs. Guy McAfee), Mrs. Temple Ellis, Ruby Ellis, Temple Ellis.

Ruby Ellis was a member of the first graduating class at Lubbock High School in 1909. Ten students were graduated at commencement exercises held in a jammed Opera House (Graves, History of Lubbock*).*

The Ellis family lost everything they owned in a fire, and Mr. Ellis became ill, so Mrs. Ellis went back to school and was a member of the first graduating class of Texas Tech University in 1926. Later, she wrote a novel, Road to Destiny, *drawing on her own experiences when she first came to Crosby County. She and Nellie Spikes co-authored* The History of Crosby County, *which has won many awards, including the Mark Twain Book Award. It has been designated an Official Historical Book of the State of Texas. Picture courtesy of The Museum, Texas Tech University; information courtesy of Mrs. Ellis' daughter, Mrs. Dan Young of Lubbock*

First Lubbock football team, 1910.

Back row: Coaches J. E. Vickers, left, and C. D. Lester, right. Courtesy of Southwest Collection, Texas Tech University

"The rush," says the note on the bottom, "where one lot a minute was sold." The car places this picture sometime in the early 1900s. The great ranches were breaking up and being turned into smaller plots. The boom was on! Courtesy of Southwest Collection, Texas Tech University

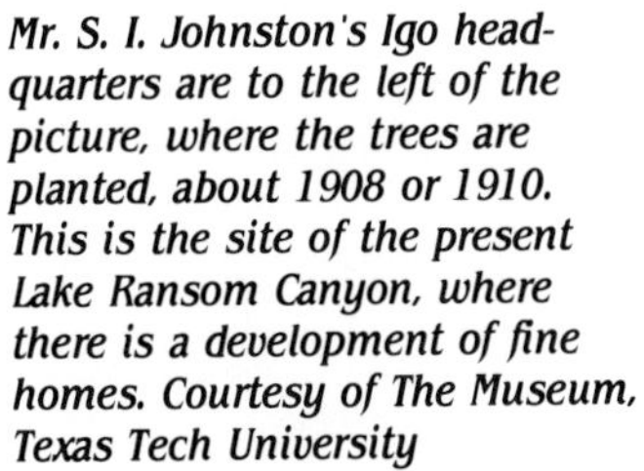

Mr. S. I. Johnston's Igo headquarters are to the left of the picture, where the trees are planted, about 1908 or 1910. This is the site of the present Lake Ransom Canyon, where there is a development of fine homes. Courtesy of The Museum, Texas Tech University

Lubbock-to-Plainview mail hack about 1910. Shortly after this time, mail started traveling by auto. Courtesy of Southwest Collection, Texas Tech University

Interior, Lubbock Iron Works about 1910. W. D. Phenix owned and operated this combination smithy and forge. The anvil at right got hard use. The smith appears to be working on a tractor seat of some kind, while in the background, a buggy waits to have its metal springs repaired. Today, in Lubbock, only one blacksmith practices—Burney Chapman—and then only by appointment. Courtesy of Southwest Collection, Texas Tech University

Burney Chapman is the only full-time farrier for hundreds of miles; he travels thousands of miles each year, shoeing horses. Courtesy of Burney Chapman; picture courtesy of Nilah Rogers

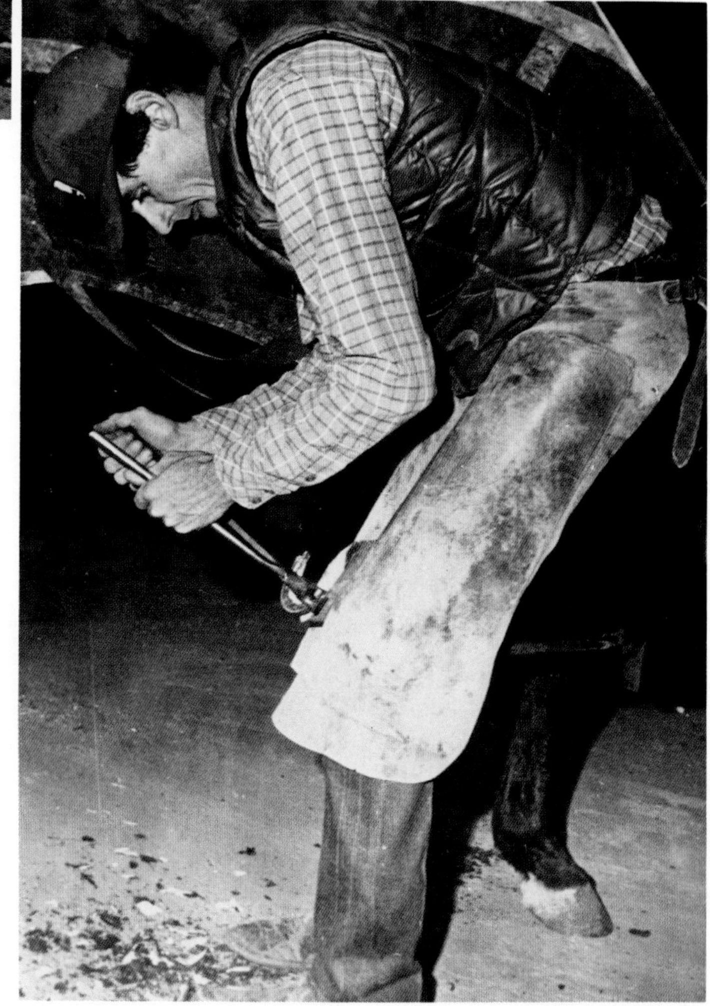

Lubbock Iron Works, about 1912. The shop stood where the old Woolworth's store was located until a few years ago on Broadway. The Lubbock Opera House, seat of local entertainment, was on the second floor. Courtesy of Southwest Collection, Texas Tech University

Lubbock loves parades! About 1912, a circus came to town. Even today, children turn out to gape at the elephants when the circus arrives, and the young lad in front of the car, at right, now probably takes his own grandchildren when the elephants march in Lubbock. The sign on the first elephant advertises "Style Dress Shop, Mrs. Van Sanders, Prop." On the second elephant, the sign reads "Tidwell & Co., Dry Goods and Shoes." Original from Mrs. A. P. Edwards; courtesy of The Museum, Texas Tech University

A water wagon in the square about 1911. There were no water mains, only windmills, and on occasion, water had to be hauled for miles. This wagon carries advertising by local merchants on its sides. In the background are two clothing stores, a barbershop, and a drug store. Courtesy of Lubbock Chamber of Commerce

W. D. McMillen's irrigation well, 1913, had a 1,200 gallon capacity. The farm was five miles northwest of the city of Lubbock. The drillers had to drill forty-seven feet to reach the water table. In 1913, a farmer could irrigate 160 acres for $20 to $25 per acre. A buyer could purchase fully equipped irrigated farmland for between $35 and $50 per acre. This picture was a postal card put out as part of a series to attract potential farmers to Lubbock. Courtesy of The Museum, Texas Tech University

On July 29, 1913, Bill Brown and his dog and wolf team passed through Lubbock, bound from Nome, Alaska, to Washington, D.C. He had already traveled 11,000 miles and had some more to go. The post office, bank, and grocery store are in the background. Courtesy of The Museum, Texas Tech University

Willard Johnson, in 1901, indicated that irrigation from underground wells might be the variable which would enable the Plains to become a fertile, profitable agricultural community (Roy Sylvan Dunn, in Graves, History of Lubbock*).*

Uncle Hank Smith dug the first well in the Lubbock area for Paris Cox while Cox went back to Indiana in 1879-80 to fetch his family to the Plains. From 1906 on, interest in drilling wells for irrigation multiplied. Some of the early wells were steam-powered by machines using coal for fuel.

This well appears to be hand-powered. In the foreground is a type of pump with the handle projecting. The mules at left are hauling pipe. The condition of the parched tree in the center shows that the driller needs to hurry and complete the job. Wells did not arrive in significant numbers until the 1940s. Courtesy of Southwest Collection, Texas Tech University

Trades Day, April 7, 1913, in the courthouse square. "The 'Trades Days'. . . reflect the cooperative spirit of the businessmen in town. Two or three times a year, usually in the summer, and for a time on the first Monday of each month, merchants declared a special sale, issued joint handbills advertising their wares, and tried to coax visitors to come to the 'Hub'" (Graves, History of Lubbock*). These were great attractions, and crowds came from as far away as 100 miles. Courtesy of Southwest Collection, Texas Tech University*

The early residence of W. L. Ellwood has the windmill and water storage tank typical of early Lubbock houses. The roof is flat, as was the case with other large homes. Courtesy of Southwest Collection, Texas Tech University

Taken by Daniels Studio in 1914, this photo shows all the automobiles in Lubbock County assembled in the square. The site is on Broadway at Texas Avenue and looks west toward Citizens National Bank. Courtesy of Lubbock Chamber of Commerce

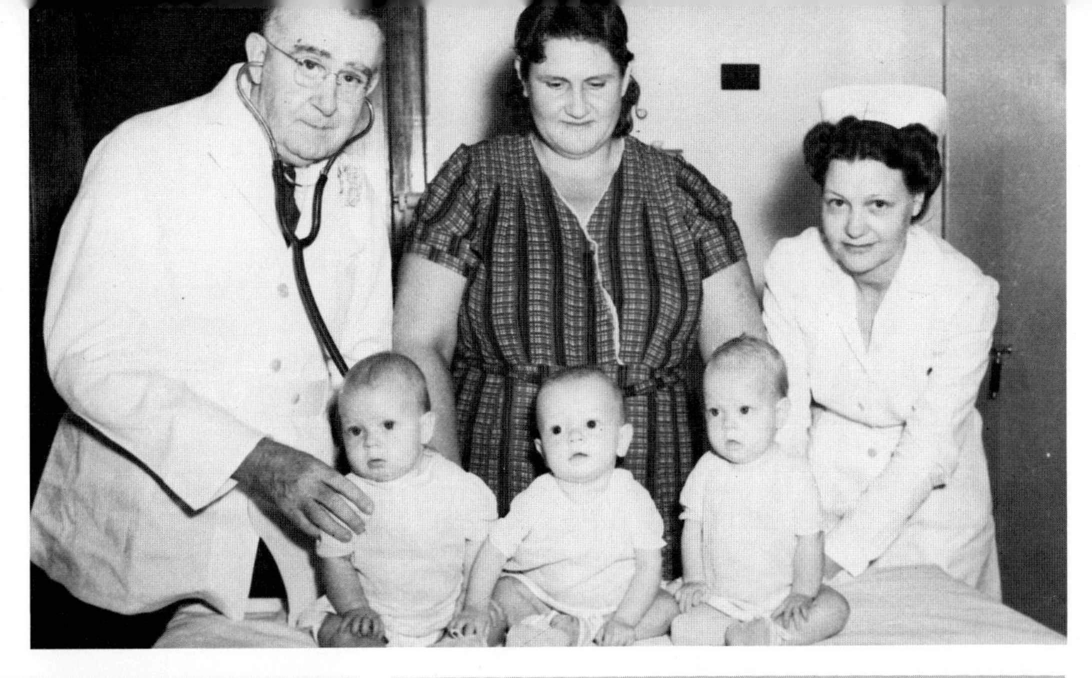

Dr. Marvin C. Overton delivered hundreds of new Lubbock citizens when he first came in 1901, then their children and their children. His book, Your Baby and Child, *became a classic with bewildered new mothers long before Dr. Spock. He had a soothing way with mothers of sick children: "There, there, Mother," he would say. Under the earpiece to his stethoscope sits the fresh carnation he put into his lapel every day until he died in 1955. Courtesy of Southwest Collection, Texas Tech University*

1918 postal card to Mrs. Jonathan Penney, Lubbock, showing Maurice Powell, a nephew of Mrs. Clark Mullican. It reads: "Say, Aunt Myrtle, please put me on your dresser so I can be seen. Lovingly, Maurice." Courtesy of The Museum, Texas Tech University

Lubbock contributed many fine young people during World War I. Here's Fiesta Bush Markham, who enlisted in the United States Naval Reserve Forces on September 26, 1918, and was discharged on November 4, 1920. She served as Yeoman First Class. Courtesy of The Museum, Texas Tech University

Lubbock

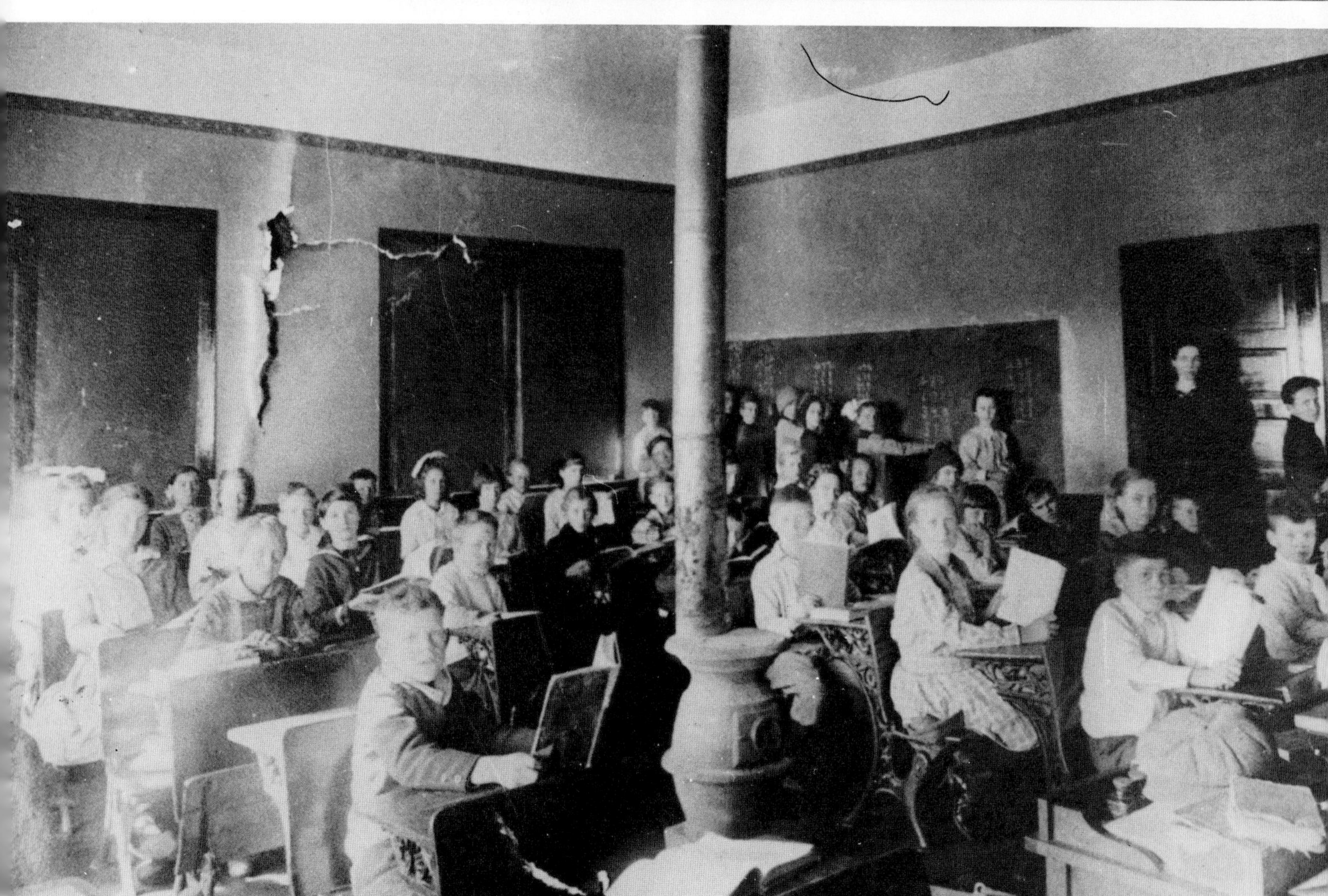

*The new Lubbock Sanitarium about 1917, at Broadway and Avenue L built by Drs. J. T. Hutchinson, O. F. Peebler, and A. R. Ponton, and later joined by Dr. M. C. Overton. Shortly thereafter, according to Graves (*History of Lubbock*), Peebler and Ponton left, and it became the Krueger, Hutchinson, Overton Clinic and Lubbock Sanitarium. Nurses' training was started almost as soon as the doors were open. Surgery rooms were on the top floor of the left wing.*

As late as 1948, the doctors were holding Sunday office hours for patients who could not come in during the week. On Saturday nights, the emergency room hummed with shootings and stabbings and other traumas resulting from over-exuberant celebrations and ongoing family feuds. Many a young physician was called to the emergency room about seven o'clock on a Saturday evening and staggered wearily home Sunday morning after an entire night of stitching up patients. Courtesy of The Museum, Texas Tech University

A Lubbock classroom in 1915. No blackboard jungle, this. The children are neat and attentive. The tops to the desks lifted to receive books and papers. Prized, well-behaved pupils were rewarded by teacher's allowing them to fill the inkwells set into the desks from a large ink bottle with a spout attached. Also, they would be allowed to stay after school to erase the blackboard thoroughly, then to go outdoors and knock the chalk dust out of the erasers.

In winter, a fortunate few got to sit near the little stove. Lubbock was a cow town, so the stove was fueled mostly with cattle droppings dried into cow chips.

All grades were in one room, and McGuffy's Reader, *with its selection of high-minded moral admonitions aimed at young minds, was the text. Pupils were called upon to recite as well as commit to memory long passages of prose and poetry. To the young students adding three-digit figures at the board, computers would have been a fantasy of the future. Courtesy of The Museum, Texas Tech University*

An early Lubbock office, probably about 1918. The telephone, typewriter, and adding machine are typical of the period. Those cracks in the wooden walls let in plenty of frigid air in the winter, so the secretary, on the right, probably could not sit too far from the stove. The posters on the walls are typical of styles during World War I. Courtesy of The Museum, Texas Tech University

This is the original Church of Christ building. Built near the old Santa Fe passenger station on Main Street in 1906, it was moved to this location about Main Street and Avenue E. Courtesy of Broadway Church of Christ

In 1912, Dr. M. C. Overton came to Lubbock as a young physician out of medical school in Louisville, Kentucky. In 1901, he built this two-story Lubbock Sanitarium. In 1920, when he joined Drs. J. T. Hutchinson, O. F. Peebler, and A. R. Ponton in the new Lubbock Sanitarium at the corner of Broadway and Avenue L, presently the home of First Federal Savings and Loan. Dr. Overton's former partner, Dr. Clayton, operated this building for several years (Graves, History of Lubbock*).*

When Dr. Clayton relinquished the building, in 1920, it became renovated as the St. Francis Hotel. Clark Smith was summoned from Texico, where he had run a successful hotel, to become the manager. The St. Francis was known all over the Plains for its fine cuisine, the result of Smith's personal trips to market and his meticulous supervision of his kitchen.

Smith's daughters, Betty Smith (Mrs. Sam) Weaver and Eunice Bondurant, live in Lubbock. The old building was in the direct path of the 1970 tornado and was subsequently razed. Courtesy of Southwest Collection, Texas Tech University

Taken in 1918, nevertheless this is a timeless occurrence on ranches around Lubbock—branding cattle. Courtesy of The Museum, Texas Tech University

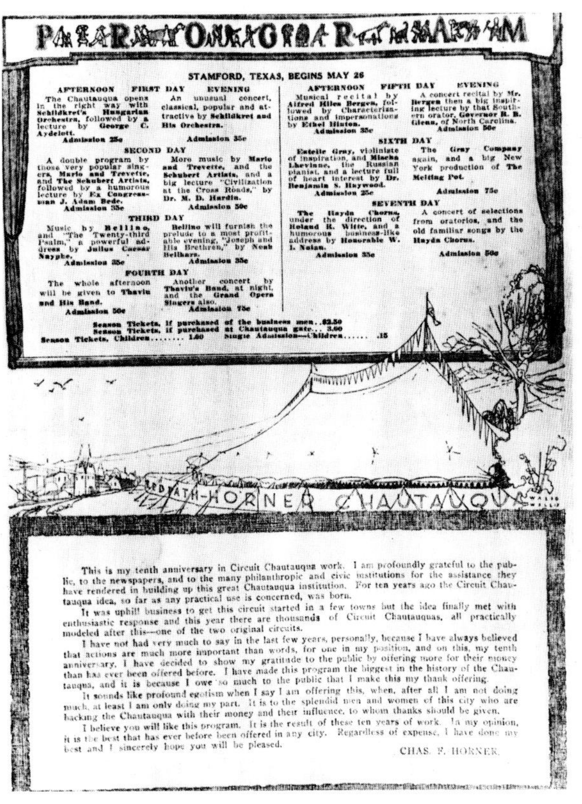

STAMFORD, TEXAS, BEGINS MAY 26

FIRST DAY

AFTERNOON — The Chautauqua opens in the right way with **Schildkret's Hungarian Orchestra**, followed by a lecture by **George C. Aydelott.** Admission 25c

EVENING — An unusual concert, classical, popular and attractive by **Schildkret and His Orchestra.** Admission 35c

SECOND DAY

A double program by those very popular singers, **Mario and Trevette**, and **The Schubert Artists**, followed by a humorous lecture by **Ex Congressman J. Adam Bede.** Admission 35c

More music by **Mario and Trevette**, and the **Schubert Artists**, and a big lecture "Civilization at the Cross Roads," by **Dr. M. D. Hardin.** Admission 50c

THIRD DAY

Music by **Bellino**, and "The Twenty-third Psalm," a powerful address by **Julius Caesar Nayphe.** Admission 35c

Bellino will furnish the prelude to a most profitable evening, "Joseph and His Brethren," by **Noah Beilharz.** Admission 35c

FOURTH DAY

The whole afternoon will be given to **Thaviu and His Band.** Admission 50c

Another concert by **Thaviu's Band**, at night, and the **Grand Opera Singers** also. Admission 75c

FIFTH DAY

AFTERNOON — Musical recital by **Alfred Hiles Bergen**, followed by Characterizations and impersonations by **Ethel Hinton.** Admission 35c

EVENING — A concert recital by **Mr. Bergen** then a big inspiring lecture by that Southern orator, **Governor R. B. Glenn**, of North Carolina. Admission 50c

SIXTH DAY

Estelle Gray, violiniste of inspiration, and **Mischa Lhevinne**, the Russian pianist, and a lecture full of heart interest by **Dr. Benjamin S. Haywood.** Admission 25c

The **Gray Company** again, and a big New York production of **The Melting Pot.** Admission 75c

SEVENTH DAY

The Haydn Chorus, under the direction of **Roland R. Witte**, and a humorous business-like address by **Honorable W. I. Nolan.** Admission 35c

A concert of selections from oratorios, and the old familiar songs by the **Haydn Chorus.** Admission 50c

Season Tickets, if purchased of the business men..$2.50
Season Tickets, if purchased at Chautauqua gate... 3.00
Season Tickets, Children........ 1.00 Single Admission—Children...... .15

This is my tenth anniversary in Circuit Chautauqua work. I am profoundly grateful to the public, to the newspapers, and to the many philanthropic and civic institutions for the assistance they have rendered in building up this great Chautauqua institution. For ten years ago the Circuit Chautauqua idea, so far as any practical use is concerned, was born.

It was uphill business to get this circuit started in a few towns but the idea finally met with enthusiastic response and this year there are thousands of Circuit Chautauquas, all practically modeled after this—one of the two original circuits.

I have not had very much to say in the last few years, personally, because I have always believed that actions are much more important than words, for one in my position, and on this, my tenth anniversary, I have decided to show my gratitude to the public by offering more for their money than has ever been offered before. I have made this program the biggest in the history of the Chautauqua, and it is because I owe so much to the public that I make this my thank offering.

It sounds like profound egotism when I say I am offering this, when, after all I am not doing much, at least I am only doing my part. It is to the splendid men and women of this city who are backing the Chautauqua with their money and their influence, to whom thanks should be given.

I believe you will like this program. It is the result of these ten years of work. In my opinion, it is the best that has ever before been offered in any city. Regardless of expense, I have done my best and I sincerely hope you will be pleased.

CHAS. F. HORNER.

While this Chautauqua program cover comes from Stamford, Texas, it represents the programs for Lubbock from 1919 to 1923. The Chautauqua tent stood on the corner of Broadway opposite the corner where the present First Federal Savings and Loan now stands.

The Chautauquas were big events: Instrumental and vocal music, pantomime, and oratory in the grand manner entertained the residents of the area. From 1919 to 1923, the Redpath-Horner Chautauqua Company came to Lubbock annually, usually for six days at a time in May. After taking its contracted percentage, the company sent the receipts to the Lubbock Chamber of Commerce. Courtesy of Southwest Collection, Texas Tech University

Plowing next to the courthouse square. This picture was taken some years after Rollie Burns and his associates had formed the Lubbock Ice and Light Company in 1909 to provide ice and power to Lubbock; the clue is the wire strung on the pole. The man on far left stands beside a plow; a horse and buggy are visible in the background. Courtesy of The Museum, Texas Tech University

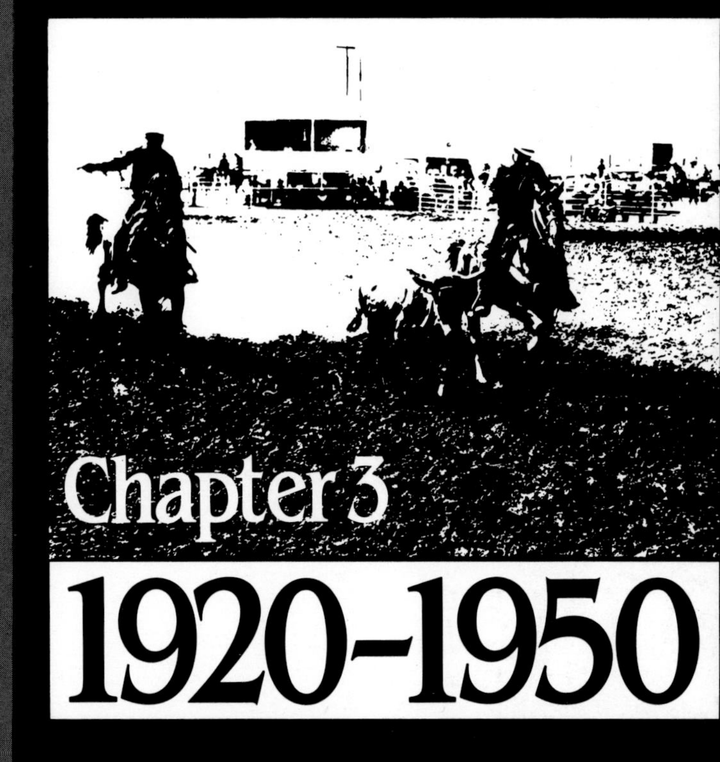

Chapter 3
1920-1950

Two boys in a cottonfield on the outskirts of Lubbock in the 1920s. Courtesy of Southwest Collection, Texas Tech University

AIR-SCAPE OF LUBBOCK

"Towns do not happen—they are built."

Ten million acres of productive farming land lies within the trade territory of the city, peopled by 63,453 white, home-owning Americans. The entire section made an increase of 91 per cent in population, according to 1920 census figures.

"OUT WEST WHERE A MAN FEELS AT HOME"

Lubbock is built for the future, with wide streets, open park areas, an extensive tree planting policy, twenty blocks of paved streets, good schools, two hospitals, fine churches, eleven wholesale houses, five railroad and six Designated State Highway outlets, a free recreation and tourist park, Golf and Gun Club, swimming parks, municipal light, water and sewer systems and a constructive and progressive type of citizen-

This is the American home of Sudan Grass, first grown in the United States on this farm in 1911. All fruits, berries, garden produce, grains, clovers, alfalfa, corn, grain sorghums, cotton, peanuts and other crops grown in Texas are successfully grown on this farm with a view to picking out the varieties especially fitted to the section.

The State Experimental Farm is located on a tract of 160 acres of land presented to State by the City of Lubbock. In 1920 there were completed 2,008 separate experi-ts, 8,000 trees distributed and advice given to more than 1,000 visiting farmers.

These are part of a series of promotional postal cards which Lubbock issued about 1920 to attract prospective new residents to the young, growing community. The attractions were numerous. One can only speculate about the safety of the pilot and photographer in the plane which took the air-scape! Courtesy of Lubbock Chamber of Commerce

Triumphantly, in 1923, after long competition with other West Texas communities, also suitors for establishment of an institution of higher education, Lubbock won Texas Technological College. The day that Governor Pat Neff signed the bill in 1923, bells rang, and Lubbock's nearly 5,000 citizens rejoiced in the streets.

In 1925, the college admitted its first students. Since that time, Texas Tech has become a university with an enrollment of more than 23,000, serving all of West Texas. Dr. Lauro Cavazos, president of Texas Technological University and the Texas Tech Health Sciences Center, recently said that of the fifty percent of the students who come from outside West Texas, fifty percent come from Dallas, Houston, and Fort Worth. From small beginnings in 1925, Tech has become a giant, serving the entire state. In keeping with their new institution of higher learning, in 1923 Lubbock citizens established the Lubbock Music Club, a little theater group, and other groups dedicated to culture.

When the Depression hit the nation, and Lubbock, neighbors pulled together. The population had reached 20,520. Churches of the town joined to feed the hungry, even though some ministers were "inclined to blame the Depression on sin and seek the remedy in religious revival" (Graves, *History of Lubbock*).

The Lubbock Loyalty Council, established in 1931, maintained citizens' confidence in Lubbock banks; consequently, Lubbock was one of the very few cities in the country with no bank failures. There was no panic.

In April 1926, the City Federation of Women's Clubs was organized. This eventually became the Lubbock Women's Club, now housed in the redesigned Plains Funeral Home at 2020 Broadway.

On September 8, 1935, sixteen young women organized the Junior Welfare League which was to affiliate in March 1954 with the Association of Junior Leagues of America. Perhaps the most noteworthy of its many charitable activities was the establishment on September 15, 1939, of the Well Baby and feeding clinic.

People learned to compromise, to make do with what was at hand. In 1935, with garments at a premium, a dressmaker complimented a customer on her lovely new gown. Fingering the material, she asked, "Where did you get that beautiful white linen?" The wearer laughed. "This material comes from fifty-pound flour sacks bleached in the sun in buttermilk." While the dress pattern business was not then the gigantic industry it later became, still, one pattern company put out a pattern to make boys' and girls' clothing from men's old suits.

In another example of trust among friends, if someone wanted to go to the movies but had no money, he would give an IOU at the box office and redeem it the next time he had ten cents.

Lubbock survived the Great Depression and was the stronger for it.

Lubbock, by then a town of 31,853, was scarcely entering the 1940s when the country was plunged into World War II. Since army pilots were coming to Lubbock to be trained in great numbers, and transient military spent time here, the United Service Organization established two bases to serve their recreational needs. Leona Gelin (Mrs. Bill) Kent was in charge of the main unit (also during the Korean conflict); Corine (Mrs. D. C.) Fair was her assistant at the East Lubbock unit.

Area towns supported the Lubbock USO. Every week, a different community would take a turn being hosts. There was a Plainview Night, a Floydada Night, and a Brownfield Night. The hosts came in cars laden to the roof with food for the soldiers. Although sugar was rationed, the area neighbors contributed their own and never asked for food stamps in return. They only wanted to share what they had with men going overseas.

Because West Texas is so vast, and because the large air base at Fort Sumner, New Mexico (just over the New Mexico line), provided little recreation for its servicemen, there was no place for off-duty men to go, so the Lubbock USO took busloads of young women in for their dances. Marguerite (Mrs. J. Hooper) Stiles had responsibility for these junior hostesses.

The Fort Sumner USO brought in the big bands: Benny Goodman, Frankie Carl, Kay Kyser, and Les Brown. Mrs. Kent recalls that Doris Day was one of the Les Brown singers. Immediately after the dance, the girls went to their dormitories. Several times each night, the chaperones conducted a thorough bedcheck, and woe betide the young lady who wasn't there! Independently organized as the Lubbock Service Organization after six months, it became a project of the Lubbock Chamber of Commerce.

During the war, food was scarce. Rationing was in effect. George Mahon, Representative to Congress from this district, wrote identical letters to Secretary of Agriculture Wickard and Price Administrator Henderson, disapproving elaborate state dinners: "Squandering food is just as bad as wasting ammunition or military equipment. Lavish dinners are uncalled for at a time when housewives scan empty store shelves for food" (*Avalanche-Journal*, January 8, 1943).

In January 1943, milk was fourteen cents a quart, Mead's large bread loaf, seven and one-half cents. Butter and cheese were rationed. Women made bandages. Dogs for Defense claimed several canine Lubbockites. The ban on drafting married men and men with children was lifted early in 1943, and on March 1, Tech instituted preflight training on campus.

After the war, Lubbock began a growth cycle which lasted into the 1960s. Returning servicemen started new businesses, new wholesale outlets sprang up, churches flourished, construction boomed. Servicemen from other parts of the country who first became acquainted with Lubbock during the war decided to return to rear their families. Lubbock was becoming a full-fledged city.

In the early 1920s, Bob Crump often hunted coyotes. These cowardly predators, which ran in packs of from five or six to around thirty, attacked yearling calves, biting off the tail. Therefore, coyotes were considered fair game. Courtesy of The Museum, Texas Tech University

Bales of Lubbock cotton, about 1920, at the McDonald gin. Courtesy of Southwest Collection, Texas Tech University

The lobby of the Nicollet Hotel in 1921. The floor was tile and the chairs were hard. Beneath coat racks on the left is a statement of the rates and rules of the house. Courtesy of Southwest Collection, Texas Tech University

Ropes school bus in the early 1920s. Courtesy of Southwest Collection, Texas Tech University

Threshing wheat near Lubbock in the early 1920s. Courtesy of Southwest Collection, Texas Tech University

Cattle on the ranch of Floyd Beall near Lubbock, about the middle 1920s. Ranchers on the Plains had much earlier gone from scrawny longhorns to whiteface Herefords. Nothing can be seen for miles and miles except more miles and miles! Courtesy of Southwest Collection, Texas Tech University

Harley Sadler draws a large crowd to his tent show, June 28, 1942. Courtesy of Southwest Collection, Texas Tech University

Harley Sadler's shows entertained more West Texans than almost any other single feature. He created the character "Toby," a carrot-topped philosopher with a touch of fun. Charles Guy, former editor of the Avalanche-Journal *writes: "Harley Sadler... brought more joy, more good clean fun, more real entertainment to more people in West Texas than any other man alive... for a quarter of a century. From 1916 to 1949, when he left show business for oil and politics, he was the most widely known and loved man from Wichita Falls to the New Mexico line and... north to the Oklahoma Panhandle."*

At sixteen, Sadler played slide trombone with a carnival. In succession, he had a tailor shop in Abilene and for a few months, studied law in Albany at a small Presbyterian college. In 1917, he became a comedian with the Roy E. Fox players. In 1923, he started his own shows.

His generosity was his downfall. He gave free lifetime passes, but eventually had to stop. Quietly charitable, he kept a meal ticket at an early "hash house," the White House Kitchen, near Tech. Says one old-timer, "No tellin' how many people ate on that ticket and didn't repay."

Always frail, but giving freely of himself and his resources, Sadler died shortly after he entered politics. He left a legacy of decent entertainment. Charles Guy writes: "On his monument should appear the words 'Toby' often spoke, 'Never, in one of my shows, has there been or shall there ever be, a word, a song or an inflection to cause a lady to blush!'"

This circa 1920 photo shows Harley Sadler in his comic character, "The Cowboy," with Wilbucks Comedians. Courtesy of Southwest Collection, Texas Tech University; photo by Theatrical Work

Harley Sadler, sometime in the mid-1920s. Courtesy of Southwest Collection, Texas Tech University

On May 28, 1890, a single family and a preacher-farmer met for the first non-Quaker religious service in Lubbock County. This picture shows the "old" Church of Christ, Broadway and Avenue N, which occupied this location from 1922 until 1950, when a large new church was built in the 1900 block of Broadway. On May 4, 1980, the church opened a new education center adjacent to the church. Courtesy of The Museum, Texas Tech University

In June 1921, the Tumble-N Pool, a private enterprise, opened on the land now Mackenzie Park. Graves writes that "some 1,500 people watched the diving exhibitions and the swimming races. Senator Bledsoe delivered the dedicatory address and the Lubbock Band played for the occasion" (History of Lubbock). Courtesy of The Museum, Texas Tech University

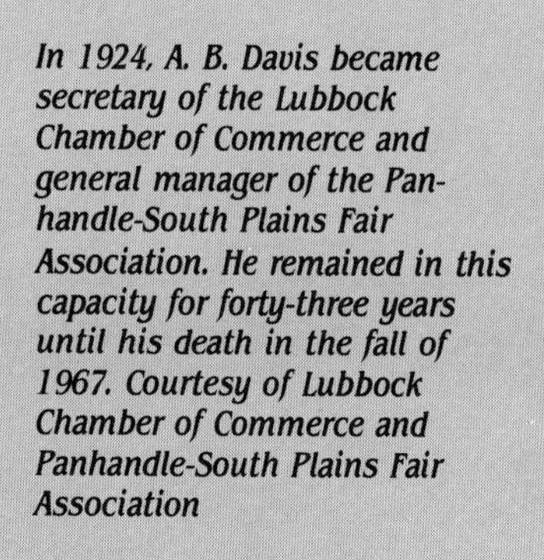

In 1924, A. B. Davis became secretary of the Lubbock Chamber of Commerce and general manager of the Panhandle-South Plains Fair Association. He remained in this capacity for forty-three years until his death in the fall of 1967. Courtesy of Lubbock Chamber of Commerce and Panhandle-South Plains Fair Association

Born in 1867 in Vermland, Sweden, John Gelin, an early Lubbock builder, lived in Chicago for twenty-five years. After a short stay in Corpus Christi, Gelin heard about Lubbock and arrived in 1917. His family joined him later.

Many early buildings bear the proud mark of his construction: the First United Methodist Church's former building at Broadway and Avenue M; the College Inn opposite the Tech campus (the first Tech girls' dormitory); the original unit of the West Texas Hospital at 1302 Main Street; and the B. E. Needles building at Fifteenth Street and Avenue H. The latter has been named as a Lubbock Historic Site. His daughter, Leona Gelin (Mrs. Bill) Kent, says that the Needles building was solidly constructed as an early filling station and garage, with a second floor built to contain parked cars. In the course of razing some property in that vicinity several years ago, construction workers were unable to tear down the building because the second floor was so solidy constructed.

John Gelin died in 1956 at the age of eighty-nine. He loved the city and has left a heritage only a skilled builder could have constructed.

John Gelin wrote to his wife, Elvira, and children, who had remained in Corpus Christi while he became established in Lubbock, March 26, 1917:

"When I got up Saturday, I went out and tried to get a job and got work on the Court House. Well, it's only $3.60 per day, but it's better than being idle. . . . I had to join the union and that was $16.00. . . board and room is high—$8.00 per week. . . . As I told you, this is a very busy place and a lot of new people are coming. There are very few women. . . and not a house or a room for rent in town.

"The Methodists hold their meetings in a shed. . . the church burned down. Next month, they start their new one, a $5,000 building. They are very attentive and friendly to strangers. . . . In general, everybody is very accommodating and nice." Courtesy of Leona Gelin (Mrs. Bill) Kent

Inez Medlock, her beau, and a Model T roadster about 1926. That's a trunk lid raised on the rear of the car. The rumble seat was yet to be thought of and flappers were yet to come. Courtesy of Southwest Collection, Texas Tech University

In November 1923, voters approved a bond issue, including $75,000 to build a new City Hall, shown here about 1929. Later, the city of Lubbock erected a fire station to the left. This building is on the site of what is now City Hall. Courtesy of Southwest Collection, Texas Tech University

—PART I—

Grammar School

Little Boy Blue .... Engleman
Edith Peek and Rebecca Quinn.

Curly Locks .... L. E. Orth
Beulah Moore (Primary Dept.)

Holiday Two Step .... Read
Edith Thomas.

Rain Pitter-Patters .... Theo Dutton
Doyle Blankenship

Dancing Flowers .... Edward Holst
Cecil, Flora and Edna Sims.

Fairy Polka .... Spindler
Bobbie Wilkinson

Les Marguerites .... La Fontain
Flora Sims

The Whispering Leaves .... Chas. Tanley
Mmes. Wesley von Rosenberg, ..., Rylander and Gelin.

Pixies Good Night Song .... A. L. Brown
Mellie Thomas

Rondoletto (C major and C Minor) .... Burgmuller
Edna Sims

The Dance of the Brownies .... E. F. Hamman
Rebecca Quinn

Edelweiss Glide Waltz .... E. F. Vanderbeck
Loyce Mills.

Summer .... Lichner
Annette Hussey

(Ten Minutes Intermission)

—PART II—

High School

The Dance of the June Bugs .... Holst
Edith and Ruby Peek

The Harp at Midnight (Nocturne) .... V. B. Aubert
Lillian Cunningham.

When the Heart is Young .... Dudley Buck
Ethel Summers

Polka Brillante .... F. Spindler
Waldene Chauncey

Sonata No. 2 G Major (Meatoso; Poco Andante Allegro Moderato) .... Bohm
Ruth Hussey and Mrs. Gelin

Chanson Des Alps (Fantasia De Concert) .... Ryder
Cecil Sims

Good-Bye .... Tosti
Mrs. Wesley von Rosenberg

Pearl and Diamonds .... Lange
Ida Lou Ellis

(a) Third Mazurka .... Ben. Godard
(b) "Home Longing" .... Jungman
Ruth Hussey.

Babylon .... M. Watson
Mr. Gelin

Les Sylphes .... Bachman
Ida Lou Ellis and Mrs. Gelin

RECITAL

Advanced Students High School

First Presbyterian Church

May 9, 1922

8:15 O'clock

Piano Duet—Polonaise .... Hoffman
Alma Spikes, Glenna Fay Grant

Chacone .... Rouber
Lois Cone

(a) To a Wild Rose .... McDowell
(b) Gavotte
Glenys Honey

Sunbeams .... Thurlow Linrance
Mary Louise Middleton

Joy of the Morning .... Oley Speaks
Katie Maude Turner

Valse .... Poldwi
Modelle Simpson

Sweet Confidence .... Dolmetsch
Irma Dalrymple

Doll Dance .... Gaetano Mercadante
Vivian Hardy

Serenata .... Tosti
Lois Nelson

The Butterfly .... Merkel
Willie Morgan

Perles et Diamants (Valse Brilliante) .... Gustao Lang
Bernice Philips

Spring Song .... Menderhou
Elizabeth Scott

March .... Holleander
Margaret Turner

In May Time .... Oley Speaks
Lillian Shelton

(a) Berceuse .... Kjerulf
(b) Music Box .... Rudolph Friml
Alma Spikes

Life's Lullaby .... Lane
Ruth Logan

Forest Elves .... Schytte
Edith Peek

in Troikes .... Tschaikowsky
Glenna Fay Grant

Petite Mazurka .... Sapellnikoff
Loys Tubbs

The Pupils and Teachers
of the
Primary and Grammar School Departments
of the
Lubbock Public Schools.
request your presence at the laying of the
Corner Stone of the
New Ward School Building
Friday, October 19
at 2:30 p. m.

In 1922, on May 9, Mrs. John Gelin's advanced piano students from Lubbock High School held a recital at the First Presbyterian Church. The program shows that many long-forgotten favorites entertained proud parents and friends. Student recitals and contests are still a strong component of Lubbock life. Not long after, in October, the Lubbock Public Schools laid the cornerstone of the new Ward Building. Courtesy of Leona Gelin (Mrs. Bill) Kent

The Xmas Store

Has a beautiful supply of gifts that last, for every member of the family.
—Christmas Spirit is not a condition of the atmosphere, but it comes rom your happy sort of good cheer. You will be happy if you make some one else happy with a gift from—

BARRIER BROTHERS DEPARTMENT STORE
"DEPENDABLE MERCHANDISE"
Save Gold Bond Savings Stamps.

I have always thought of Christmas time a good time; a kind, forgiving, generous, pleasant time; a time when men and women seem by one consent to open their hearts freely; and so I say: God bless Christmas."—Charles Dickens.

Christ is won't to catch every man in the way of his own craft—Magians with a star, fishers with fish.—St. Chrysostom.

A good conscience is a continual Christmas.—Benjamin Franklin.

—Mid-Season finds us well prepared with the needful articles at the lowest price. Try our "WUNDER" Hose for the school boy or girl.

K. CARTER'S STORE
"The One Price Store—Always the Lowest"
Phone 434

HULEN K. FINLEY, M. D.
Chronic Diseases a Specialty

KATE P. CASTLEMAN, D. C.
Chiropractic-Masseur, Assistant

CHIROPRACTIC MASSAGE, ELECTRICAL HEAT AND WATER TREATMENTS A SPECIALTY
In the Prevention and Treatment of Deformities, Nervous and Chronic Diseases
Phone 790. Security State Bank Bldg. Lubbock, Texas

REMEMBER WHERE YOU CAN GET THE BEST IIN GROCERIES
ED. WILSON'S CASH STORE
"The Odd Cent Store" PHONE 828

We are Headquarters for—
TOYS, DOLLS and EVERYTHING

LUBBOCK VARIETY STORE
(Across Street from Ritz)
W. B. Hilton Mrs. J. L. Chaw

The First Methodist Church, South

Cor. Ave. M and Broadway

REV. C. N. N. FERGUSON, PASTOR

REV. E. E. ROBINSON, D. D. .... Presiding Elder, Lubbock District
REV. GEO. L. WATERS .... Missionary to Japan
(Supported by Busy Man's Bible Class)
W. C. RYLANDER .... District Lay Leader

W. K. DICKINSON, Sr. .... Chairman Official Board
SAM T. DAVIS .... Secretary-Treasurer
A. B. ELLIS .... Incidental Treas.
JAS. L. DOW .... S. S. Supt.

SAM F. COOPER, Supt. Senior Dept.
H. W. STANTON, Supt. Intermediate Department.
MRS. H. W. SIMS, Supt. Junior Department.
MRS. J. H. RHEA, Supt. Primary Department.
MRS. W. E. KITTRELL, Supt. Beginner's Department.

Present enrollment 1280. Our goal for the year 2000 and attendance 1300.
MRS. W. C. RYLANDER, President Woman's Missionary Society.
J. T. INMON, Charge Lay Leader.
MISS BLANCHE BEAN, President Epworth League.
JOHN GELIN, Choir Leader.
MRS. MAMIE NEAL, Organist.

SUNDAY, DECEMBER 17, 1922

Morning Service 10:58
Doxology.
Inovocation.
Hymn.
Memory Reading.
Glora Patri.
Scripture.
Announcements.
Offertory.
Subject: Sermon by Rev. C. N. N. Ferguson "Rebuilding Fences and Repairing Bridges."
Invitation Hymn.
Benediction.

Evening Service 7:00
Hymn.
Scripture.
Prayer.
Offertory.
Hymn.
Sermon, Rev. C. N. N. Ferguson, subject "Personal Devil. Are His Headquarters in Lubbock."
Invitation Hymn.
Reception of Members.
Benediction.
Greeting Strangers.

Announcements
Laymen's Meeting 3:00.
Intermediate League at 4:00, Mrs. Ferguson, Supt.
Senior League at 6:00.
Preaching at 7:00.
Prayer Meeting, Wednesday evening at 7:15.
Junior League and Junior Missionary Society, Friday evening at 1:11; Mrs. F. R. Pickens, Supt.

FIVE HUNDRED AND TWENTY-THREE HOMELESS CHILDREN WERE TURNED AWAY FROM THE METHODIST ORPHANAGE THIS YEAR.
NO ROOM FOR THEM

Where are they? We do not know. What is your responsibility in this matter? You will answer this question one way or the other during the glad Christmas time.

A score of carrier pigeons will be sent to various sections of the State so that they can bring your answer back Home. Nine of the birds, one for each of the presiding elders' districts in the West Texas Conference, will be sent to San Antonio and when the final count is made from all the charges in the districts, early on the new morning, the birds will wing their way back home with your answer to this big question. May it be a glad message for the kiddies at the Home, for two hundred and sixty pairs of eyes of the orphans in the Home will be looking for the Home coming of the birds. FIVE HUNDRED AND TWENTY-THREE pairs of ears of the homeless orphans will be listening in to get your answer. Will you make it a glad New Year's message for them?

Their guardian angels are waiting to see what the answer of our great Church will be to the orphan's cry.

Brother Pastor, in presenting the cause of the orphan during Christmas time, be as earnest and as interested as if it were your little boy or girl that was homeless. They are His little lambs.

With faith in our Good Father and confidence in a great Church we believe that there is a better day ahead for our great Orphanage.

We covet your most earnest prayers and liberal support.

SEND ALL CHECKS TO THE METHODIST ORPHANAGE, WACO, TEXAS

Gift Suggestions for a Man—
—From a Man's Store
Initial Handkerchiefs, Brown Capeskin Gloves, Silk Neckwear, Pajamas, Comfy Slippers, Bath Robes, Silk Hosiery.

L. E. HUNT & CO.
Clothiers
"We Will Make Right That Which Is Not Right"

"100 per cent Dentistry at Pre-War prices."

DR. FERGUSON
Office Conley Building
Phone 535

Engraved Christmas Cards
Visting Cards
Announcements
Invitations

We have a complete stock of Wedding Invitations, Announcements and Calling Cards. We print or engrave, just as you choose.
THE AVALANCHE
Phone 14.

For Choice, Fresh Meats and the best of Groceries
——trade with——
H. W. SIMS, Phone 52

We are everlastingly trying to provide our customers with the best milk. Clean—Absolutely!

MEDLOCK'S DAIRY
PHONE 405

For Choicest of Meats, Fish and Oysters, Call
THE CITY MEAT MARKET
PHONE 812
On Broadway, in Front of The Lendo

THE CITIZENS NATIONAL BANK
The Bank of Personal Service
No accounts too small to receive our careful attention

A December 17, 1922, First Methodist Church program lists, on the back, some of the local merchants.

Note the title of Dr. C. N. N. Ferguson's sermon: "Personal Devil: Are His Headquarters in Lubbock." There was no question in the minds of ministers and many of their congregations that the devil was ever-present in Lubbock, and they devoted their efforts to stamping him out at every opportunity. Founded by devout Quakers and with early Church of Christ missionaries, as well as other denominations arriving monthly, Lubbock quickly established the fundamental nature of her religion. The churches were adamant about the evils of drink, and this kept Lubbock nominally dry until the late 1950s. Courtesy of Leona Gelin (Mrs. Bill) Kent

Lubbock Woodworks, established by John Gelin, builder, right after the Depression years. It blew away during the 1970 tornado and was replaced by a modern building. They are still in business. Gelin built furniture for churches as well as the churches themselves. In addition to these pews, he also made a minister's chair, guest chair, and communion table. He made a gift to the church of the last three items. Courtesy of Leona Gelin (Mrs. Bill) Kent

The exact location of this 1920 house, designed and built by John Gelin, is unknown. However, it was probably located around Avenue R, near the old Groce Furniture Company. Its stucco, ruffles, and embellishments were not typical of Lubbock architecture, but were probably built to custom specifications. Courtesy of Leona Gelin (Mrs. Bill) Kent

This is the Hotel Lubbock under construction in 1925. It was red brick with white wood trim and featured a portico topped with iron railings, probably designed by the Lubbock Iron Works. The center of all Lubbock organized social activity until the building of the Hilton Hotel, it still stands at 102 Broadway as the Pioneer Retirement Hotel. Courtesy of Southwest Collection, Texas Tech University; photo by Daniel Studios

Lubbock has always loved community get-togethers to visit with neighbors and exchange the latest news. Food is always an integral part of "neighboring," and since there was little shade at this early 1920 picnic, everyone, even children, wore hats. Courtesy of Southwest Collection, Texas Tech University

The Fort Worth and Denver Railroad station under construction in 1928. Wyatt C. Hedrick, a Fort Worth architect, designed the building, which was constructed at a cost of $46,889. It served Lubbock until it was abandoned in 1953.

In 1973, it was purchased and restored by 1974 as a restaurant utilizing most of the original features. Since then, the Lubbock Urban Design and Historic Preservation Commission, a city governmental agency, has designated it a Historic Landmark, one of seven such designations in the city. Courtesy of Randy Henson, City of Lubbock Planning Department; courtesy of Southwest Collection, Texas Tech University

Looking west on Broadway in the early 1920s. Courtesy of Southwest Collection, Texas Tech University

REX

This early 1920s meat market was owned and operated by Fred W. Sims and his wife and son, who are standing behind the counter. The minutes of the Lubbock City Commission for 1924 show that Sims, along with two other butchers, Ed Ainsworth and J. A. Luster, and the city health officer, Dr. G. C. Castleberry, were prime movers in a successful move to create an official food inspector to prevent sale of uninspected meat and to force butchering houses to comply with Texas sanitary laws (Graves, History of Lubbock*).*

The huge refrigerator in the background was maintained with block ice furnished by a local ice manufacturer. Sims used the roll-top desk in the background in his business. The fans and the clock and calendar on the wall were typical of mercantile and market establishments of the day. Courtesy of The Museum, Texas Tech University

The old Warren Bacon residence about 1928. The windmill and the water tower behind the house were features of most of the grander houses in Lubbock at this time. Courtesy of Southwest Collection, Texas Tech University

Right
Some of the Lubbock County Democrat workers for Al Smith's campaign for the presidency in 1928.

Front row, left to right: Judge Charles M. Nordyke, Franklin D. Brown, Hill Stewart, Walter F. Schenck, W. O. Stevens, L. A. Howard, William W. Campbell, Jesse M. Marshall.

Back row, left to right: James H. Goodman, Emil L. Klett, Pink L. Parrish, Jesse C. Levens, two unknown names, Clark M. Mullican, Walker C. Rylander, George E. Lockhart, Benjamin Kucera, J. Harvey Moore, Robert H. Bean, Charles C. Triplett. Courtesy of Southwest Collection, Texas Tech University

Left
Completed in 1928, the old Burlington Railroad Depot at Nineteenth Street and Avenue G fell into disrepair some years later. It served for some years as a salvage depot and a brickyard. In mid-1973, restoration began from original plans and specifications found in some old papers, and it opened in June 1976 as The Depot Bar and Restaurant. The Lubbock Design and Historic Preservation Commission has designated it their first Historical Site and placed a bronze marker on it.

Many customers, some from out of town, have fond memories of the old station. One man's father, an early architect, drew part of the plans which are now framed on the wall. Another's father shipped out to Fort Sill in Oklahoma during World War II from the station. Still another recalls that his father and mother left for their honeymoon from there. This shows the restored station in 1979. Courtesy of James Ferguson

A fine, old Packard convertible, about 1928. If you had one now, you could retire on the proceeds of selling it. Courtesy of Lubbock Chamber of Commerce

The first West Texas Hospital, built when the old Overton Sanitarium shut down operations as a hospital. Dr. C. J. Wagner had been a partner with Dr. Overton in this enterprise. Begun in 1920 at Main and Avenue L, at a cost of $125,000, it opened in March 1922. Drs. Baugh, Craven, Hall, Stewart, Starnes, and Wagner composed the original staff. As was the case at the Lubbock Sanitarium, this hospital almost immediately started training nurses (Wagner interview, Baugh interview in Graves, History of Lubbock*). Courtesy of The Museum, Texas Tech University*

Interior of the Lubbock National Bank in the late 1920s. C. E. Maedgen is behind the counter. Senator W. H. Bledsoe, instrumental in obtaining Texas Tech University for Lubbock, stands at the counter. Courtesy of Southwest Collection, Texas Tech University

Orderlies at the then-new Lubbock Sanitarium about 1927 or 1928. Courtesy of Southwest Collection, Texas Tech University

Around 1928, looking east on Broadway, Lubbock's busiest street. The handsome Bacon house is at left. Courtesy of Southwest Collection, Texas Tech University

W.R. McGill, first district judge in Lubbock County, when Lubbock was still part of the fiftieth district. Lubbock was fortunate not to suffer the wild lawlessness prevalent in New Mexico, Arizona, and Oklahoma. Courtesy of Southwest Collection, Texas Tech University

The Lindy Needle Club, about 1928. The women of the community met in the home of one of the members and usually served lunch. At the time this picture was taken, at least four other needle clubs existed in Lubbock. The photographer took this picture in the yard of Mrs. H. D. Woods, 2113 Seventeenth Street, in Lubbock. Courtesy of Southwest Collection, Texas Tech University

Texas Tech

Paul W. Horn, the first president of Texas Technological College, greeted the student body in the 1926 yearbook, *La Ventana:*

"You have been our comrades in a great adventure this year—the establishment of the Texas Technological College. You have helped us to lay the foundations for a new institution, for an institution that will endure for many years to come. You have had a part in shaping its policies and in establishing its traditions.

Such an opportunity as we have had comes to people but once in a lifetime.

It is a magnificent country in which our college is located. . . . a region of magnificent distances, of far-flung horizons, of deep canyons, of lofty far-arching skies.

Everything that is done on these West Texas Plains ought to be on a big scale. It is a country that lends itself to bigness. It is a country that does not harmonize with things little or narrow or mean. Let us make the work of our college fit in with the scope of our country. Let our thoughts be big thoughts and broad thoughts. Let our thinking be in world-wide terms.

Let our affections, likewise, and our sympathies be as broad as the world is wide. Let us strive to exclude from our lives that which is petty, mean, ignoble."

The Administration Building under construction, 1925. Courtesy of Southwest Collection, Texas Tech University

This photograph, November 11, 1924, shows the laying of the cornerstone of the Administration Building at Texas Tech.

A sealed box placed in the cornerstone contained the following objects: newspapers; by-laws of the local lodge of Masons, a list of members of the local lodge, and members of the Grand Lodge participating; names of members of the board of directors of Texas Technological College; names of the governor and lieutenant governor, a photograph of the governor, and a roster of the members of the House and Senate; a certified copy of the bill establishing the college, with the history of its passage; the brief of Lubbock filed with the Locating Committee when it offered a site for the college; coins and other souvenirs furnished by individuals; and a list of the board of directors of the West Texas Chamber of Commerce. Courtesy of Southwest Collection, Texas Tech University

The carillon in the tower of the Texas Tech Administration Building. The bells were a gift from Ruth Baird Larabee of Kansas City, whose father had been an early landowner around Lubbock, and she lived in Lubbock for several years. She donated the land to the university to furnish the bells. Majestic and sonorous, they ring out over the Tech campus in summertime concerts. Courtesy of Dorothy Rylander

Tech Administration Building, photographed in 1933. Courtesy of Southwest Collection, Texas Tech University

The first commencement exercise, May 30, 1927. Left, Dr. Paul Horn, first president of Texas Tech; right, Dr. William Bizzell, president, University of Oklahoma, who made the first commencement address. Courtesy of Southwest Collection, Texas Tech University

Senator William H. Bledsoe, a leading member of the early Lubbock Bar Association, wrote and introduced into the upper chamber in Austin, Senate Bill 103, which provided for the establishment of Texas Technological College in Lubbock. On February 10, 1923, Governor Neff signed the bill into law. Courtesy of Southwest Collection, Texas Tech University

First commencement, 1927. Dr. John C. Granberry, foreground; Dean Gordon in the background. Courtesy of Southwest Collection, Texas Tech University

The Texas Tech Student Dairy Barn, about 1925. Courtesy of Southwest Collection, Texas Tech University

A close view of the residence of the first president of Texas Tech, Dr. Paul Horn, in 1925. This cream-colored, stucco, Spanish-style house with red tile roof houses the Ex-Students' Association in 1980. Courtesy of Southwest Collection, Texas Tech University

President's home, Tech campus, May 31, 1925. This building still stands at the corner of Nineteenth Street and University Avenue, and currently houses the Ex-Students' Association. Courtesy of Southwest Collection, Texas Tech University

A student bottles milk at the Tech Dairy at Texas Tech, about 1940. How long it has been since anybody's seen one of those pink milkbottles! Courtesy of Southwest Collection, Texas Tech University

The Texas Tech Chemistry Building in 1925. Courtesy of Southwest Collection, Texas Tech University

The Textile Engineering Building was one of the first three buildings on the Tech campus. Courtesy of Southwest Collection, Texas Tech University

Charlie, wife Selma, and baby Snookie. He was the first cook at the College Inn, 1925. Courtesy of Southwest Collection, Texas Tech University

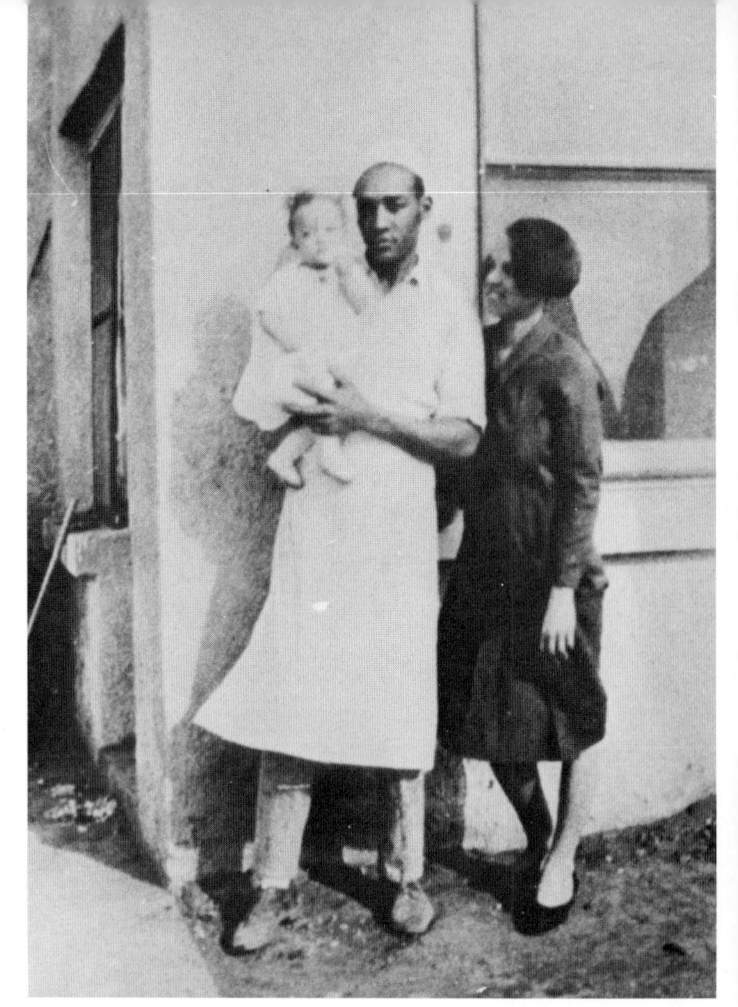

Mrs. Erie Studerman, 1925, first housemother at College Inn, the women's dorm. Courtesy of Southwest Collection, Texas Tech University

Mr. Spence in front of the Tech Novelty Store, 1925. The store was located in one corner of the College Inn, at Fifteenth and University (then College Avenue). Courtesy of Southwest Collection, Texas Tech University

DEDICATION

TO A MAN, WHO BY HIS PERSONAL EXAMPLE OF CLEAN LIVING, HAS TAUGHT US THE VALUE OF TRUE MANHOOD.

TO HIM, AS A COACH, WHOSE EFFORTS HAVE INSTILLED US WITH A FIGHTING SPIRIT THAT MAKES THE SCARLET AND BLACK FEARED AND RESPECTED THROUGHOUT THE SOUTHWEST.

TO HIM—PETE W. CAWTHON—WE DEDICATE THIS LA VENTANA OF 1932.

Pete Cawthon, coach of the Texas Tech football team from February 4, 1930 to August 23, 1941. Courtesy of Etta Lynch

Under Coach E.Y. Freeland, Captain Hurley Carpenter scored the first touchdown on Texas Tech's gridiron when Tech played St. Edwards on October 9, 1926. The first team was dubbed "The Matadors," but because when he arrived in 1930 Coach Pete Cawthon put bright red uniforms on his teams, the name "Red Raiders" quickly supplanted the first designation. Courtesy of Southwest Collection, Texas Tech University; Daniel Studio photograph

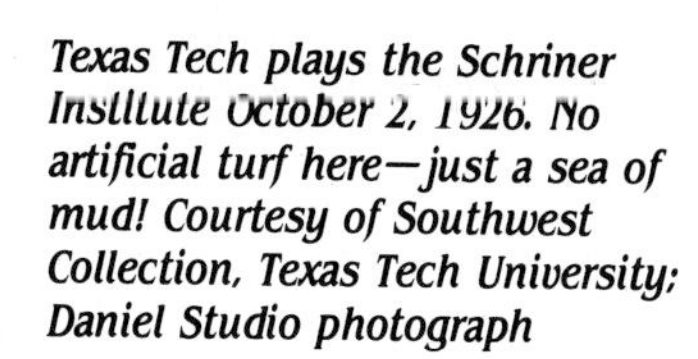

Texas Tech plays the Schriner Institute October 2, 1926. No artificial turf here—just a sea of mud! Courtesy of Southwest Collection, Texas Tech University; Daniel Studio photograph

This unfortunate Texas Tech football player can't seem to make up his mind which sport to pursue! Courtesy of Southwest Collection, Texas Tech University

The Red Raider on his horse, Happy VI-II. Every few years, Tech students vie to become the new Red Raider. In his scarlet costume, black hat, and mask, he is a striking sight as he gallops out to lead the Tech Red Raider football team onto the field and to circle the field at every touchdown. Courtesy of Texas Tech University

The Clifford B. and Audrey Jones Stadium looking west at the junction of Fourth Street and the Brownfield Highway, during a Tech football game. The playing surface is sunk below ground level. From September until the end of the season, football reigns in Lubbock. Courtesy of Lubbock Chamber of Commerce

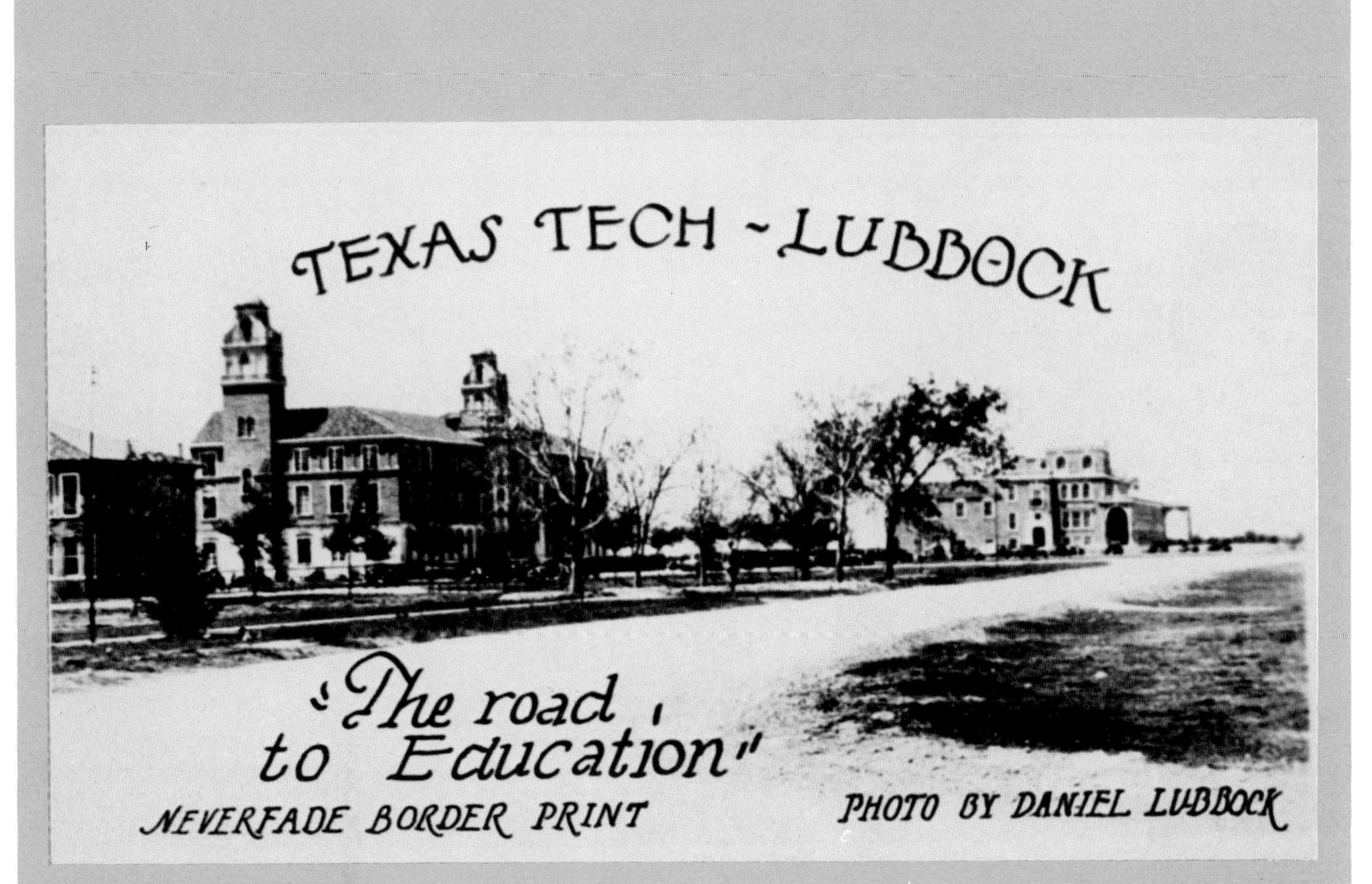

Tech campus about 1930. In 1930, Coach Pete Cawthon "turned to beautifying the Tech campus. He talked the athletic council into paying his football players a few dollars a month for helping him, and he grabbed a shovel or hoe and worked alongside them.

"They began two new baseball fields. They started four new tennis courts.... Long, back-breaking hours went into sodding the football field. Pete passed the word to the townspeople that he needed trees, any kind, and he would come and get them. Pete and his wagon loaded with trees became a familiar sight.... He planted hedges, flowers and grass; then, he hauled 300 yards of manure to fertilize them." (Lynch, Tender Tyrant*). Courtesy of Southwest Collection, Texas Tech University*

Dr. Clifford B. Jones, longtime Texas Tech president, during the 1940s. Courtesy of Southwest Collection, Texas Tech University

Tech women about 1938 wore these costumes to pursue their athletic activities. At left, Faye Hodge (Mrs. P. T. Glazner); others are unidentified. Courtesy of Southwest Collection, Texas Tech University

Playful students have been known to put detergent into the fountain at the Broadway entrance. Broadway is in the foreground, with University Avenue running horizontally, left to right, from south to north. The old College Inn was just out of the picture to the left, on the street then known as College Avenue. Courtesy of Texas Tech University Public Information Center; courtesy of Lubbock Chamber of Commerce

Archivists Mike Hooks, left, and Janet Neugebauer, right, are pictured at work in the oral history section of the Southwest Collection, a center for research and for preservation of historical materials. The oral history section contains recorded reminiscences of living and departed Lubbock citizens— some of them early cowboys and early settlers— whose work and lives furnished a foundation for the Lubbock of today.

A recent acquisition of the Southwest Collection consists of the complete papers of Congressman George Mahon, who donated his Congressional papers upon his retirement. Along with the papers of Judge Marvin Jones, these records preserve sixty years of continuous political life. Courtesy of Southwest Collection, Texas Tech University

This bronze statue of famed humorist Will Rogers on his horse, Soapsuds, stands at the end of the main entrance to Texas Tech. Executed by Electra Waggoner Biggs and the gift of Amon Carter of Fort Worth, this statue has become a community landmark. According to Tech, except for the Peter Hurd mural it elicits more national inquiry than any other feature of Tech.

When time came to place the statue, Will was to be placed with Soapsuds' nose facing into the western sunset. However, visitors approaching from the east entrance, by the fountain at University and Broadway, would not have received a particularly hospitable welcome from Soapsuds, so instead, Will and his horse face northwest.

The Tech Administration Department is in the background. Courtesy of Texas Tech University Public Information Center

The Texas Tech University campus, looking northeast, with Nineteenth Street in the foreground. The low building at left, next to three high-rise dormitories, is the then-new athletic dining room. The dome of the Auditorium-Coliseum can be seen in the upper left. In the center, far distance, grain elevators rise on the horizon. The law school is immediately out of the picture to the left, on Nineteenth Street. Courtesy of Southwest Collection, Texas Tech University

Christmas in Lubbock has been an important occasion since early days. The many churches in Lubbock celebrate the season as a Christian festival. In addition, open houses and parties add to the festivities. The Carol of Lights at Texas Tech epitomizes the season. Several weeks before the holidays, lights glow along the periphery of campus buildings, as shown here in 1979 on the Textile Engineering Building. At a night carol ceremony, students and townspeople gather to see the lights turned on. Courtesy of Texas Tech University

The Depression years coincided with some of the worst dust storms ever seen on the South Plains. While this tractor is a later model, the devastation of the land is typical of the era. But in the early 1940s, the establishment and proliferation of irrigation wells helped turn the Lubbock area into the fertile agricultural region it is today. Courtesy of P. Barth Cooper

The 1930 Lubbock Police Force

Behind the motorcycle at left, C. E. Luce. Left to right, front row: John LeMond, David "Pop" Davidson, unidentified chief (may have been Chief May), Randolph Rampy, Arlie Rush, unidentified. Bill Mabry stands by the motorcycle at right.

Back row, left to right: Judge W. E. Inmon, J. J. Dillard, O. T. Lindsey (?), Don Reeder (later chief), George Eubanks, Grady Harrist (later sheriff), Joe Wilson (?), Tom Cannon (?), Jess Levens, Judge Dupree. Courtesy of Dr. Billye Coker Levens, Mrs. Ola Peveto, and Police Chief J. T. Alley

H. A. Davidson in his office. By 1930, the old, tall telephone had been replaced by a "modern" hand set. Courtesy of Southwest Collection, Texas Tech University

In April 1931, the present Lubbock High School was completed at a cost of $650,000 (Graves, History of Lubbock*). The Goedeke Library, the former main library, occupied the space where the park was then but in October 1980, moved to its new branch on Quaker Avenue at Loop 289. Courtesy of Lubbock Chamber of Commerce*

Remember the roadster with the rumble seat? This picture stirs fond memories for those lucky enough to have lived in Lubbock in the 1930s. Courtesy of Southwest Collection, Texas Tech University

Like the first pioneers, this Lubbock hunter found abundant game on the South Plains in 1931. Courtesy of Southwest Collection, Texas Tech University

Cotton pickers in the early 1930s in Lubbock County. Later on, they were supplanted by machinery which greatly increased the crop yield. Courtesy of The Museum, Texas Tech University

Heavy rains in the Lubbock area, 1941. Courtesy of Southwest Collection, Texas Tech University

Cotton wagons wait their turn at the Lubbock Gin, 1932. Courtesy of Southwest Collection, Texas Tech University

About 1939, Eleanor Roosevelt spoke at the Lubbock High School Auditorium under the auspices of the American Association of University Women. Courtesy of Southwest Collection, Texas Tech University

Senator Tom Connally, who served in the United States Senate from 1929 until after World War II, is shown during a 1932 visit to Lubbock. The three-piece, white suit was especially spun and woven for him by the Texas Tech Textile Engineering Department; there were at least two others like it. A suit similar to this but made of cotton duck, manufactured from South Plains cotton, is presently in the Museum at Texas Tech. Courtesy of Southwest Collection, Texas Tech University

Interior of a Lubbock grocery store about 1932. One can find still-familiar brands on the shelves. Quaker Oats containers are at upper left, and under those boxes are some familiar condiment containers. The bins in front of the counter contain dry foods: peanuts, rice, macaroni, and dried beans. Courtesy of The Museum, Texas Tech University

HN HALSEY
UG STORE
DRINK
Coca-Cola
ANN SHER N
ANIS MOR
GS FOR TH GLE
S&Q
LOTHIERS
OLLMAN'S
BROWN'S
HAT SHOP
BOSTONIAN
FREEMAN
MEN

Broadway street scene looking east in the 1940s. John Halsey's drug store was a favorite gathering place after dances for a late soda. The old Kress building, at far right, is presently a Good Will store. This looks like a Saturday, when everybody from the surrounding area came into Lubbock to shop. Courtesy of Southwest Collection, Texas Tech University

A group of Dunbar School children during the early 1940s. Courtesy of Southwest Collection, Texas Tech University

In 1913, the Reverend Edwin Weary served Episcopalians of Lubbock as missionary curate. Later, a small congregation built a wooden church at the corner of Sixteenth Street and Avenue Q. It still stands, having served various purposes through the years. In 1941, feeling the need for expanded quarters, St. Paul's broke ground for its present building at Sixteenth and Avenue X. In the early 1970s, a new parish hall joined the north side of the church. Until that time, Seaman Hall, on Avenue X, south of the church, had served as combination Parish Hall, music recital hall, and student service center. St. Paul's has always had its share of Tech's student population, since it is only one block from the campus. Courtesy of Lubbock Chamber of Commerce

Ice storm in Mackenzie park in the early 1940s. Courtesy of Southwest Collection, Texas Tech University

Will Rogers, Jr., at left, and movie actress Rochelle Hudson are shown during an early 1940s trip to Lubbock. Courtesy of Southwest Collection, Texas Tech University

Reese Air Force Base

Reese Air Force Base came into existence as Lubbock Army Air Field on June 23, 1941. The 2,000 acres of land in which Reese is located were donated by citizens of the Lubbock area for the construction of the training facility. The field officially opened in late 1941, and training of aviation cadets began in early 1942. With the end of World War II, the base was closed and served as a veterans housing and a training site for the National Guard.

The base was reactivated on August 1, 1949, with the 3,500th Pilot Training Wing moving to Reese from Barksdale AFB, Louisiana. The wing was redesignated as the 64th Flying Training Wing on October 1, 1972.

Reese AFB is named in honor of First Lieutenant Augustus F. Reese, a native of nearby Shallowater, Texas, who was killed in action at Cagliari, Sardinia, May 14, 1943, while on a mission in a P-38 to destroy a railroad supply train.

In April 1961, Reese AFB was named as one of the seven original Air Training Command bases to conduct undergraduate pilot training. Good flying weather permits an average 345 flying days a year.

The years have seen many changes at Reese. Pilot production has increased, thousands of new pilots have received new wings, and many new buildings have been constructed; but the mission of Reese has remained the same—to train top quality military pilots (information courtesy of Reese Air Force Base Office of Public Affairs).

Two groups of Lubbock Army Air Field personnel took a break in the 1940s. Courtesy of Reese Air Force Base Office of Public Information

Lubbock Army Air Field, when the flight section was part of the army, about 1943. Courtesy of Southwest Collection, Texas Tech University

4

Relations between Reese Air Force Base and the Lubbock and area communities have always been mutually beneficial. Reese personnel involve themselves in every facet of life in the communities. Here, two members of the Reese Color Guard lead local school children in the pledge of allegiance to the flag following a presentation on the history of the flag and the courtesies rendered to it. Courtesy of Reese Air Force Base Office of Public Information

Reese Air Force Base new Wing Headquarters, completed in 1975. The three-story complex houses the wing commander and his staff, as well as the legal office, finance office, public affairs, and the contracts division. Courtesy of Reese Air Force Base Office of Public Information

Cadet Reza Pahlavi (left) and his instructor pilot, Air Force Captain John E. Thompson, Jr., emerge dripping from the dunk tank after being tossed in to commemorate the cadet's September 1978 first solo flight in the Cessna T-37 jet trainer. Cadet Pahlavi, the Crown Prince of Iran, underwent undergraduate pilot training at Reese between July 1978 and March 1979. Courtesy of Reese Air Force Base Office of Public Information

Reese Air Force Base's new Undergraduate Pilot Training/ Instrument Flight Simulator building, the largest building on the base. Courtesy of Reese Air Force Base Office of Public Information; photo by Larry Houston, LSI

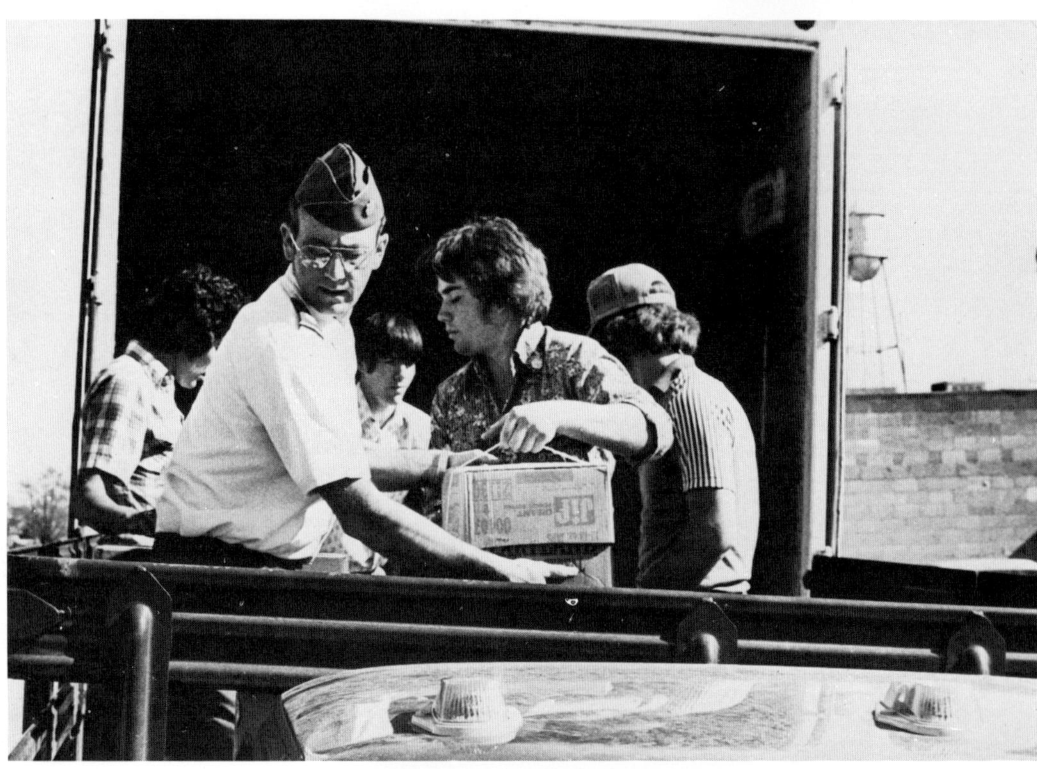

Here, Reese personnel help load supplies destined to help the tornado relief effort in Wichita Falls, Texas, in April 1979. Courtesy of Reese Air Force Base Office of Public Information

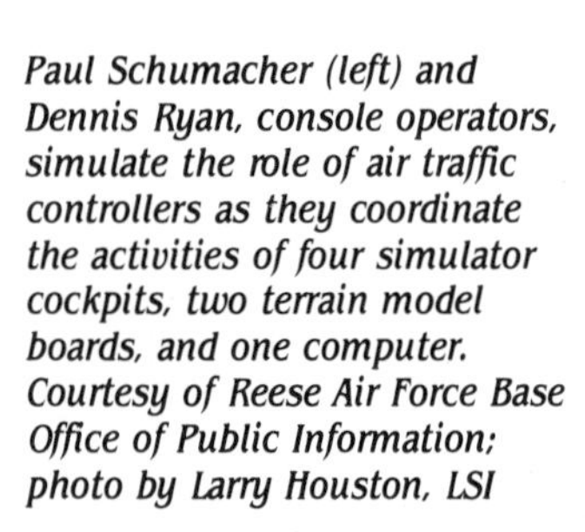

Paul Schumacher (left) and Dennis Ryan, console operators, simulate the role of air traffic controllers as they coordinate the activities of four simulator cockpits, two terrain model boards, and one computer. Courtesy of Reese Air Force Base Office of Public Information; photo by Larry Houston, LSI

The Reese AFB water tower looms over building T-1, original wing headquarters. Since this picture was taken in the early 1950s, a new facility houses the wing commander and his staff. Courtesy of Reese Air Force Base Office of Public Information

About 1950, this is the old Reese Hospital. Courtesy of Reese Air Force Base Office of Public Information

Soldiers march during World War II. The brick street is an excellent example of early street construction, much of which still remains in as good condition as when it was laid in the twenties. No potholes here. Courtesy of Southwest Collection, Texas Tech University

Sergeant Alee Simmons during World War II. Courtesy of Southwest Collection, Texas Tech University

Carefully selected junior hostesses from the community helped entertain cadets in local training at a dance in the Hilton Hotel ballroom about 1943. Courtesy of Southwest Collection, Texas Tech University

A local department store helped keep up morale during World War II with this window display. Lubbock, like other communities, was proud of her men and women in uniform. Courtesy of Southwest Collection, Texas Tech University

The Boy Scouts contributed to a scrap drive held in the early 1940s in Lubbock to aid our war efforts. Courtesy of Southwest Collection, Texas Tech University

Saturday night at the Lindsey Theatre, the most popular place in town in the 1940s. Courtesy of Southwest Collection, Texas Tech University

Margaret Turner, longtime women's department editor at the Avalanche-Journal, *had both journalistic and personal style. After beginning her newspaper career in 1929, she became women's editor in 1934. In January of 1963, she left the newspaper and now lives in California. Courtesy of Southwest Collection, Texas Tech University*

The J. T. Krueger home, 2703 Nineteenth Street, Lubbock, on January 15, 1946. One among many fine homes built in Lubbock in the late 1930s and early 1940s, its Corinthian columns face the south campus of Texas Tech University. The architectural firm of Haynes and Strange worked with Mrs. Krueger on the design and execution of the house, implementing ideas she crystallized as a result of taking an architecture course at the university. Courtesy of Southwest Collection, Texas Tech University

The Halsell brothers about 1945. E. L. is on the right, Harry on the left. Their grandfather came west with his family, and eventually the family staked claim in the vicinity of the present Muleshoe area, on the Plains northwest of Lubbock. Courtesy of Southwest Collection, Texas Tech University

Meadowbrook Golf Course when it was first laid out in the 1940s next to Mackenzie Park. Courtesy of Southwest Collection, Texas Tech University

Many Lubbock women have been avid golfers. That's the clubhouse on the grounds of Meadowbrook Golf Course, next to Mackenzie Park. Courtesy of Southwest Collection, Texas Tech University

Dr. J. T. Hutchinson in his office in the 1940s. Builder of the Lubbock Sanitarium with two other physicians in 1917, he later limited his practice to otolaryngology, starting in 1909. None of his patients ever remembers seeing him without his head mirror. The picture on the desk is his son, Tom. Courtesy of Southwest Collection, Texas Tech University

A meeting of the Panhandle District Medical Society in the Early 1940s

Left to right, front row: Dr. J. P. Lattimore, two unidentified Amarillo physicians, Dr. Julius T. Krueger.

Left to right, back row: Dr. M. M. Ewing, Dr. W. L. Baugh, Dr. Martin Benson, an unidentified physician. Courtesy of Southwest Collection, Texas Tech University

Dr. C. J. Wagner in the early 1940s. Dr. M. C. Overton induced him to come here because he spoke German and there was a growing German population in and around Lubbock. Courtesy of Southwest Collection, Texas Tech University

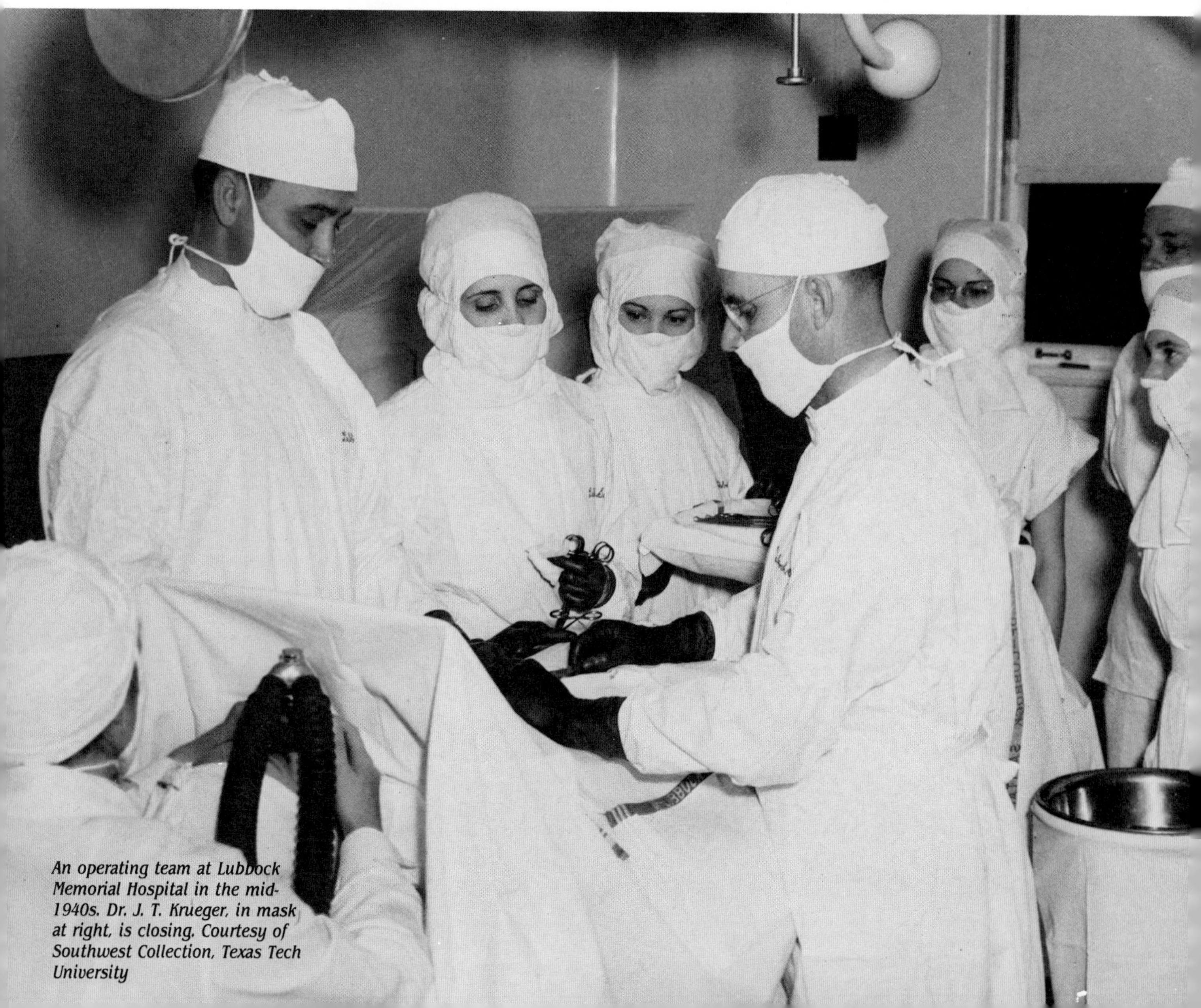

An operating team at Lubbock Memorial Hospital in the mid-1940s. Dr. J. T. Krueger, in mask at right, is closing. Courtesy of Southwest Collection, Texas Tech University

A Lubbock wedding in the 1940s. Courtesy of Southwest Collection, Texas Tech University

The Plains Funeral Home on Broadway later was renovated to become the present Lubbock Women's Club. It is the center of many social activities year-round. Courtesy of Southwest Collection, Texas Tech University

CHERISHED
BUDDY HOLLY

Chapter 4
1950–1980

In 1980, fans from all over the world still visit Buddy Holly's grave in the City of Lubbock Cemetery. Elvis Presley has been quoted as saying that Holly was a great influence on his style, and Holly's impact on the youth of his generation continues today. Courtesy of Buddy Holly Memorial Brochure

Lubbock native Buddy Holly sprang into musical prominence in the mid-1950s. His music was a unique blend of folk, western swing, country, and bluegrass, and he set toes to tapping at a time when country music was gaining national popularity. Just as his career was reaching national prominence, he died in a February 1959 plane crash. Since his death, Holly's music has come into worldwide vogue. His music is particularly popular in England. Courtesy of Lubbock Chamber of Commerce

Shown here is a twelve-inch bronze replica of Grant Speed's seven-foot monument to Buddy Holly. The unveiling took place September 7, 1980, in the Memorial Civic Center in Lubbock. The group which commissioned the statue includes Waylon Jennings, Snuff Garrett, Larry Corbin, Jerry Coleman, and former mayor Dirk West. Along with Holly's grave, this is the focal point of pilgrimages by Holly fans from all over the world. Courtesy of Buddy Holly Memorial Brochure

After the World War II decade of the 1940s, Lubbock grew at express speed. By 1950, Lubbock's population had increased 125% from 1940, to 71,747. Due to returning servicemen who established new businesses and because of rapid new home construction, Lubbock began to expand and diversify. Many servicemen, stationed during the war at Lubbock Army Air Field, or transient, were impressed by the community and its friendliness, and they returned to live permanently. They found a neighborly population in a clean city filled with churches and schools, a city where they wanted to rear their growing families.

During the 1950s, Texas Tech expanded rapidly, due in part to the GI bill, which gave financial aid to returning servicemen. In turn, this created a community within a community. Also, Tech's expanded enrollment created a demand for goods and services. Buoyed by a burgeoning economy, Lubbock citizens embarked on a series of community projects designed to make up for lost time. With the expanding city limits, shopping malls sprang up like mushrooms in outlying areas. Manufacturing, wholesaling, and all the industries connected with satisfying the needs of the population established themselves.

However, this rapid growth proved to be a mixed blessing. In the 1960s Lubbock lost no momentum. Rather, the opposite occurred. By 1960, Lubbock contained 128,691 people and suburban sprawl spread the city into what had been cotton fields. In 1952, Thirty-Fourth Street was still in the country and only beginning to develop as a commercial street. Development of new houses took the form of spotty clusters, and to some extent, the city became fragmented. As businesses moved out to the periphery, downtown Lubbock's growth slowed. Undercapitalized businesses went out of business and some rivalries over market areas occurred. At times, it seemed that the old neighborliness might be in danger.

No longer a small community, Lubbock began to attract more industry and newcomers from other parts of the country. "Why," indignantly sputtered one lady in a quiet neighborhood, "do you know, when I go out, I have to lock my doors!"

In April 1970, Lubbock voted a bond issue for civic improvement, but fate intervened. On May 11, 1970, about 9:20 p.m., a killer tornado struck the west side of the city, skipping violently over the southeast corner of the Tech campus. It uprooted trees and, only a few blocks east of Tech, hit with deadly force. Proceeding northeast, it carried everything in its path. Heavy tables and chairs were sucked out of the private club on the top floor of the First National Bank building; they were found the next morning more than a mile away near Guadalupe Park—or what remained of it. The tornado killed twenty-six people and injured scores. Shards of glass fell from glassfaced buildings in a lethal shower on motorists below.

The city mobilized quickly. Surgeons rushed to emergency rooms to treat the wounded. Hospitals turned on emergency generators. Ambulance tires, running over glass, quickly blew out, but tire dealers and service stations came to the rescue, replacing tires to complete the runs. Because of disruption of the water supply, farmers around Lubbock loaded water trucks with well water and trucked it in to hospitals and distribution centers.

The next day, again in crisis, Lubbock neighbors came to each others' rescue. The community mobilized food supplies and set up clothing stations in Guadalupe Park, the area hardest hit. The Red Cross brought in additional truckloads of clothing. Once again, friends drew together to a common purpose in disaster to support each other in common need.

Bulldozers cleared land of rubble, citizens replanted trees, and Lubbock's wounds began to heal. The United States government gave matching dollar-for-dollar funds for urban renewal. Almost immediately, the Committee for the Seventies formed to enlist knowledgeable community leaders in leading the city into the decade.

With due respect to those who suffered irreparable loss of family and property, Lubbock turned this natural disaster to benefit. The beautiful Memorial Civic Center, built on the site of some of the worst damage, is dedicated to the memory of those lost. The Lubbock International Airport exists because of this rebuilding, as does the new George M. and Helen Mahon library at 1306 Ninth Street, next to the Memorial Civic Center. As one civic leader said, "Isn't it a shame that it took a tornado to accomplish all this!"

Moving along on the surge of civic pride and cooperation that the disaster engendered, Lubbock began to boom. By this time, the population had increased to 149,101 in the city and to 179,295 in Lubbock County. A mysterious "Mr. X" appeared in November 1972 to determine data on the city's population and economy, and in March 1973, Texas Instruments officially announced plans to locate in Lubbock. Company president J. Fred Bucy was reared in Tahoka, just south of Lubbock, and he recalls that during the Great Depression, "nobody had any money and we all ate our share of turnip greens." Many in West Texas share his sentiments: "Growing up in a small town made the difference, but growing up in a small town in West Texas made the complete difference" (*Avalanche-Journal*, May 4, 1980).

Other industries contributed to Lubbock's growth at a time when the rest of the nation was in economic decline. Meat packing, chemical manufacturing, building supplies, and other industries connected with the housing industry growth came into Lubbock. They led to increases in personal services, restaurants (fast-food franchises flooded the town as more people started to eat out), and banks. Family-connected services increased due to the influx of new families. Oil, agriculture, general business, retailing, and business services sprang up. In the last half of the 1970s, energy supply became a worldwide problem, and Texas Tech has addressed itself to it.

The West Texas area is known as the breadbasket of the country. Tech and the United States Department of Agriculture have combined to set up a laboratory to study soil moisture and plant stress. In water-short countries, farmers must use what moisture is available to produce at the same level as areas with more water. Tech's Center for Energy Research operates a Solar Energy Project at Crosbyton, thirty minutes east of Lubbock. It is unique in the United States, located in advantageous territory where the sun shines most of the year in unpolluted atmosphere.

Lubbock's Committee for the Eighties has set goals for the city. They have established committees on cultural affairs, agriculture, the spirit of Lubbock, Lubbock's economy, education, recreation, and entertainment, government and taxation, transportation (intra-city and inter-city), and municipal facilities and services. They have sponsored Town Meetings where citizens can be heard.

Lubbock goes into the 1980s with flags flying!

About 1953, the firm of Crenshaw, Dupree, and Milam. Left to right: C. C. Crenshaw, Jr.; C. C. Crenshaw, Sr.; George W. Dupree; James H. Milam. Senator W. H. Bledsoe, instrumental in obtaining Texas Tech for Lubbock, was a member of this firm. Courtesy of Southwest Collection, Texas Tech University

In 1954, the state of Texas approved the operation of a private educational institution which would teach students from kindergarten through college. Thus, Lubbock Christian College, affiliated with the Church of Christ, came into being.

The elementary school operated for three years. Then, in September 1957, with sixteen faculty members and 110 students, the school became a junior college. In 1972, the school became a fully accredited college.

Presently, 1,500 students are enrolled in programs ranging from liberal arts to technical and vocational fields. Dr. Harvie Pruitt, a native Lubbockite, was selected president in 1966. Courtesy of Lubbock Chamber of Commerce

In 1917, the original Methodist church burned. Completed in 1918 under the supervision of John Gelin, the solid structure shown here was used until 1955, when the congregation built their "Cathedral of the West," one-half block south of the sanctuary at Broadway and Avenue M. The Reverend H. I. "Hi" Robinson was pastor here for many years.

This building was directly west of the old Lubbock Memorial Hospital. Many a Lubbock baby, born there, was christened here. Courtesy of Leona Gelin (Mrs. Bill) Kent

The Lubbock Municipal Airport in the early 1950s. Courtesy of Southwest Collection, Texas Tech University

Bernie Howell (Walter Burnett Howell, Jr.) was a popular Lubbock entertainer during the 1940s through the 1960s. He came to Lubbock in the early 1940s to play piano and organ on the radio and went on to have a TV program later. He played at all sorts of social functions. When Preston Smith was inaugurated governor, Bernie and his three female violinists, the "Triolins," played for an inaugural party. This smiling portrait of Bernie in the 1950s shows his typical grin. He died in Lubbock on April 23, 1978. Courtesy of Southwest Collection, Texas Tech University

Joseph Alvin Chatman, M.D. (right), shaking hands with Ralph Brock (left), is honored at a testimonial dinner on April 26, 1963. Dr. Chatman came to Lubbock from practice in Mexia, Texas, in 1939. Owner and medical director of Chatman Hospital, almost immediately he plunged into community activities: He was a director of the Negro Boys Club, a member of the Masonic order, a Red Cross director, and was active in medical circles. In 1960 and 1961, Governor Price Daniel appointed him to the White House Conferences on Aging and on Youth. Governor Daniel describes Dr. Chatman as "a great humanitarian whose broad interest and talents helped to make Texas a better place to live." He died January 12, 1967. Courtesy of Avalanche-Journal

Monterey High School, at the corner of Indiana Avenue and Forty-Eighth Street, was built in 1955 and 1956. It serves a large section of Southwest Lubbock. This picture depicts it about 1958, looking west. The residential area was built on land that contained cotton before 1950. Indiana Avenue runs north and south, just west of the athletic field. Courtesy of Lubbock Chamber of Commerce

The new First United Methodist Church stands at the corner of Broadway and Avenue M. Built in 1955 on the site of the old Methodist church, it boasts the second largest rose window in the world, which was shipped from England in sections, aboard the Queen Mary, *then assembled and installed here. Courtesy of Lubbock Chamber of Commerce*

On the left, Lubbock Municipal Auditorium opened in 1952, adjacent to Lubbock Municipal Coliseum. Until the advent of the new Civic Center, all large cultural events were held in the auditorium. The coliseum is the site of Texas Tech basketball games, trade exhibits, circuses, rodeos, and many other entertainments. Courtesy of Lubbock Chamber of Commerce

Effie Wilson was one of many civic-minded women who worked diligently for the community. The daughter of M. V. Brownfield, founder of the neighboring town of Brownfield, she married Roscoe Wilson, a Lubbock attorney and first vice-chairman of the board of directors of Texas Tech. When the Altrusa Club, a local women's service organization, selected her as Woman of the Year in February 1960, the list of her accomplishments filled two newspaper columns and ranged from service with the community arts to quiet assistance to individuals.

Mrs. Wilson was intensely interested in preserving the heritage of Lubbock and the surrounding area and was directly responsible for obtaining the Eclipse windmill now in the Water Exhibit at the Texas Tech Museum. She died December 13, 1979. Courtesy of Frances Brownfield Christman; courtesy of the Avalanche-Journal

Vera Maxey and some of the ladies who sold Lubbock women their clothes at Hemphill-Wells department store in the 1950s. The occasion is her retirement as buyer of ladies' ready-to-wear. Mrs. Maxey worked for the store from August 9, 1929, until July 1, 1957. This picture was taken May 1, 1957.

Left to right: Pauline Waugh, Mrs. Claude Hale, Lois Copeland, Ruth Snell, Ann Baze, Elizabeth Walton, Velma Hardin, Rhea Caffey, Dorothy Wilhite, Mrs. McGruder, Gladys Custer, Laura Tippett, Mae Hall, Sally Goodwin, Beulah Mitchell, and Mrs. Cook. Mrs. Maxey is seated, wearing a corsage. Courtesy of The Museum, Texas Tech University

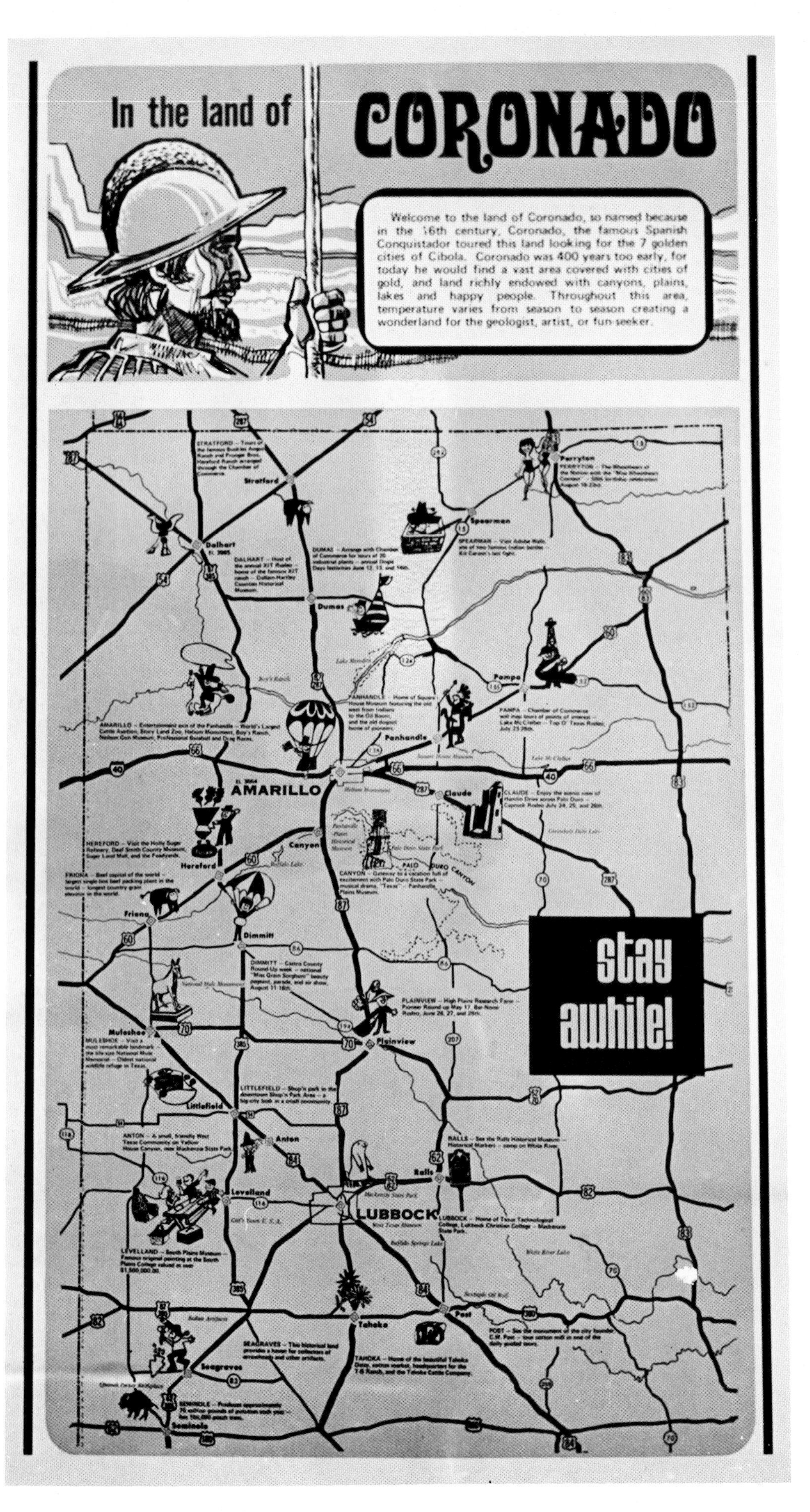

A Chamber of Commerce poster at the Lubbock Airport in the 1950s and 1960s shows Spanish trails during the time of Coronado. Courtesy of Lubbock Chamber of Commerce

Monterey Shopping Center in the 1960s. On Fiftieth Street, this was one of the earliest of such large centers in the rapidly expanding suburbs of residential Lubbock. Courtesy of Lubbock Chamber of Commerce

Lubbock Municipal Airport in the 1960s, before the new Lubbock International Airport was built nearby. Courtesy of Lubbock Chamber of Commerce

CHAPTER 4: 1950 - 1980

Skyline of Lubbock, Texas, about 1965. The earth, whose abundance made the city possible, lies in the foreground, waiting for the seed to produce another year's bountiful crop. The spires of the First Methodist Church at right are next to the Metro Tower, then the old Pioneer Hotel, now a retirement home. Courtesy of Lubbock Chamber of Commerce

CHAPTER 4: 1950 - 1980

The law school at Texas Tech. Professor Reed Quilliam, who was in the Texas Legislature when the law school was established in 1966 and has been associated with it almost from its inception, says:

"The strength of the school... will continue to be dedication to the practical training of students to equip them to practice law in this part of the country." In February 1980, the law school's Moot Court Team won first place in the National Moot Court Competition in New York City. Courtesy of Texas Tech Public Information Center

Left
Buffalo Lakes in the 1960s, before its redevelopment. Since the turn of the century, it has been a recreation spot for Lubbock residents. Boating, fishing, and swimming are popular, and some people have built cottages along the shore (left). Courtesy of Lubbock Chamber of Commerce

On January 2, 1969, Governor Preston Smith made his first inaugural address. A graduate of Texas Tech, he served in the Texas Legislature, then became lieutenant governor and later served two consecutive terms as governor. His family is seated at his right.

Governor Smith has spoken highly of Lubbock's assets: "Throughout Lubbock's history, the city has been fortunate to have produced or attracted people who have provided tremendous leadership. Texas Tech's establishment in 1925 brought with it. . . enormous cultural and economic impact. For many years, especially since irrigation was established in the 1940s, Lubbock County has been one of the outstanding agricultural counties in the nation. Over the past twenty years, Lubbock County has become a major producer of oil and gas. Perhaps Lubbock's people are the area's greatest resource. They are devoted, intelligent, energetic, enthusiastic, and willing to undertake any project beneficial to this area or to the state. My closing reminder is this: Cities do not happen—people build them." Courtesy of Southwest Collection, Texas Tech University

In 1969, Jim Prather, boss of the famed OS Ranch thirteen miles southeast of Post in Garza County, an hour's drive from Lubbock, organized the OS Ranch Steer Roping and Art Exhibit. Since then, it has become an annual two-day event in October, attended by visitors from Texas and neighboring states, who fly in for the event. Cowboys and ropers take part in arena events: steer roping, calf roping, team roping, barrel racing, and cutting horse competition. Western artists donate their artworks for auction. Barbecue and all the trimmings are served from a forty-foot barbecue pit. On Sunday, the ranch holds an oldtimers' breakfast and an open-air church service in the chinaberry grove where C. W. Post and Garza County ranchers planned the original county organization. In this picture, two cowboys work in perfect tandem to rope a steer. From the Avalanche-Journal

Historical Costume Collection

The Historical Costume Collection at The Museum, Texas Tech University, demonstrates the evolution of dress in West Texas from the simple styles of the Quaker settlers to the recent attire of the 1960s. Fashion evolves in cycles and dramatizes its time and function, and this collection displays the transitions of life in the South Plains. In the late 1890s, haute couture began to trickle into Lubbock on freight wagons from Amarillo, Fort Worth, and Colorado City. With the advent of the sewing machine, dressmakers solicited business. In addition, women on the South Plains could order ready-made dresses from Montgomery Ward in Chicago as early as the 1880s, and from Sears' first catalog in 1897 (information courtesy of Betty Mills, curator, The Historical Costume Collection, Texas Tech Museum).

About 1890, women began to feel the need to lighten their layers of garments in order to become more active. This 1892 beige wool challis dress has a lined, boned, fitted basque (waist). Under the puffed sleeve, a basic undersleeve held form. The wrists and front of the dress are composed of brown silk ruching. Typical attire for young businesswomen at the time, the dress is worn with gloves, a silk beret with a brown velvet bow, and high-laced, brown shoes with beige uppers. Gift of Mrs. John J. Gill; modeled by Mrs. Charles Pemberton; courtesy of The Museum, Texas Tech University

*Designed in France and purchased from Sanger Brothers in Dallas, this 1884 wedding gown was rumored to have cost $500. "Colonel C. C. Slaughter, a cattle baron of the Free Range Era in West Texas, ordered this gown for his eldest daughter, Minnie, for her marriage to Dr. George Thomas Veal" in that same year. Model Sally Slaughter is the great-great niece of Mrs. Veal (*The Museum Journal*). Gift of Mr. and Mrs. George Slaughter; courtesy of The Museum, Texas Tech University*

Charles Dana Gibson immortalized this skirt and blouse in the first decade of the twentieth century. His Gibson Girl, modeled after the famous Virginia belles, Irene and Nancy Langhorne (later Lady Astor), set the style which reached even to the South Plains in 1900. The black wool skirt has a slight back train, a graceful manipulation of which may have given a glimpse of the taboo ankle.

Women were beginning to become active in business by the early 1900s. Furs were expensive, so a small fur muff served well to protect a typist's hands from the piercing winds of severe South Plains winters. Gift of Bonnie Dysart and Mrs. C. B. Haynes; modeled by Mrs. George Stinson; courtesy of The Museum, Texas Tech University

On September 26, 1912, Ruby Barron married C. Fred Litton at home. A modiste in Dallas, Texas, created this beautifully detailed gown entirely by hand—one of the last rapidly vanishing handmade dresses. Detailed with hand-tucked bodice and scroll-designed, satin-covered cording, the gown's train is weighted with hidden chains covered with both cotton and satin casings. Even the lace on the slip is hand-appliqued; the seams are handbound. Gift of Mr. C. Fred Litton; modeled by Mrs. Walter Taylor; courtesy of The Museum, Texas Tech University

In 1912, Mrs. W. C. Rylander wore this dress. Elaborately beaded, with silver metallic embroidery on filet net, the three-piece blouse, skirt and tunic represent the Directoire style favored by women who preferred a more slender silhouette than had been in fashion during the first decade of the century. Gift of Dorothy Rylander; modeled by Mrs. J. Knox Jones; courtesy of The Museum, Texas Tech University

During the four years of World War I, the fashion industry took a back seat to industrial production geared to a wartime economy. After the war, the ankle emerged, thanks to the influence of French couturiers.

On September 15, 1920, when Ethel Teague married the Reverend Ernest C. Raney, she wore this reindeer tan wool broadcloth suit which cost $150 at the time. Mrs. Raney wore the suit again in 1970, on the occasion of their fiftieth wedding anniversary. Gift of Mrs. E. C. Raney; modeled by Mrs. Derry Harding; courtesy of The Museum, Texas Tech University

In 1911, McCall's *magazine contained a series of articles entitled "How to Succeed as a Stenographer," "The Successful Tea-Room," "The Woman Florist," and "The Real Estate Agent." This 1912 braid-trimmed, snuff-colored ottoman suit epitomized the "liberated" woman of that year. The severity of the tailoring is typical of the time, but an ecru net blouse, velvet hat, and fur muff lend a feminine air.*

This Sanger Brothers suit, or its counterpart, sold in 1912 for $12.75 and a liberal bonus of trading stamps if ordered by mail. Gift of Mrs. C. B. Haynes; modeled by Mrs. Grover E. Murray; courtesy of The Museum, Texas Tech University

In 1927, Mrs. W. H. Bledsoe chose this white formal net gown embroidered with baroque pearls over silver lamé for Governor Dan Moody's inaugural ball in Austin. Mrs. Bledsoe's husband was a state senator and largely responsible (as member of the locating board) for the establishment of Texas Tech in Lubbock in 1925. Gift of Department of Clothing and Textiles, Texas Tech; modeled by Dr. Mary Elizabeth King

This 1969 pearl-gray, flowing chiffon ball gown is a design by Helen Rose of California, twice Oscar-winning designer for the stars. The dress is a perfect example of the classic elegance of that year. The Empire bodice is encrusted with jeweling and enhanced by crystal tulips and solid beading. On January 20, 1969, Mrs. Preston Smith, wife of the newly elected governor, wore it in Austin for the first of the inaugural balls given in connection with Governor Smith's two terms. He was the first Lubbock resident so elected. Gift of Mrs. Preston Smith; modeled by Mrs. Howard Davison; courtesy of The Museum, Texas Tech University

This basic salt-and-pepper wool tweed suit represents the typical pared-down style of 1950. World War II had made women even more mobile and introduced thousands into wartime jobs which they continued after the war. Gift of Mrs. O. Brandon Hull; modeled by Mrs. Mike Sanford; courtesy of The Museum, Texas Tech University

On June 20, 1965, when Jane Underwood married Dr. Jack Henry, she wore this lace-panelled bridal gown complemented with a pillbox hat, a fashion made famous by President John F. Kennedy's wife, Jacqueline, and a flowing, silk net train. Second-day dresses were no longer in style in 1965 as they were in the late 1890s, but bridal gowns were no less elaborate. Courtesy of Mr. and Mrs. Harris Underwood and The Museum, Texas Tech University

Left to right: Betty Rhea Moxley in a bright red day dress, about 1900. Elizabeth Bertram, in a midnight blue poiret twill traveling suit, 1916, gift of Mrs. D. Burns. Rita Isham in a navy blue crepe evening gown with amber jeweling, 1925, gift of C. Fred Litton. Mrs. James Morris, in a black wool broadcloth winter street costume, 1908, gift of Margaret McClure. Mrs. Jack Shanklin, in a rose-beige pompadour print with puce silk trim, 1891, gift of Mrs. Carl M. Weber; this is a typical second day dress favored by brides then. Courtesy of The Museum, Texas Tech University

Mae Simmons, distinguished educator, spent twenty-nine years with the Lubbock Public Schools, sixteen of them as principal of Ella Isles Elementary School. She always directed her work at elevating the standards of her race and helped many a needy family and many a bedraggled, unfortunate child.

Her honors in the community have been many. She was a member of the Lubbock Planning Council, the Community Center Council, the Lubbock Cancer Society, and the United Fund. She served on the boards of the YWCA, YMCA, The Boys Club, The Girls Club, The Day Nursery and The Child Welfare Board. On June 9, 1963, a city park with a pool and other recreational facilities was dedicated and christened Mae Simmons Park.

"Teaching," she said, "is a mission and a good teacher must be dedicated to her profession."

She lives in Houston. Picture courtesy of Southwest Collection, Texas Tech University; legend courtesy of Avalanche-Journal

A feed lot outside Lubbock... the modern counterpart of the open range of the past. Courtesy of Lubbock Chamber of Commerce

Lubbock calls itself "The Chrysanthemum Capitol of the World." In the fall, myriads of rust, gold, purple, white and yellow 'mums dot the city in colorful display. Courtesy of Lubbock Chamber of Commerce

A prairie dog family in Prairie Dog Town in Mackenzie Park. When the first settlers came to the Plains in the 1890s, these furry little rodents owned the prairies, along with coyotes, antelopes, and buffalo. They were considered a nuisance, since horses often stepped into the holes dug in prairie dogs' subterranean tunnels and broke legs.

When they became threatened with extinction, the city rounded up several pair and fenced them in the park, where they stayed fenced for several years; but in the last few years they have dug their way out and are ruining the adjoining Meadowbrook Golf Course.

The city receives requests from all over the world and has, in fact, shipped many pairs abroad to zoos. They are engaging little creatures, sitting upright at the door guarding the entrance. At the first sign of danger, the guard chitters away in shrill tones and the families dive into the apartment. Courtesy of Lubbock Chamber of Commerce

An oil refinery on the South Plains. The number of wells in and near Lubbock is increasing rapidly. Courtesy of Southwest Collection, Texas Tech University

May 12, 1970. A Mobile Red Cross Disaster Services food van, serving Lubbock citizens who were wiped out in the tornado the night before. Courtesy of Lubbock Red Cross

May 12, 1970. The night before, a devastating tornado struck portions of central and northeast Lubbock. Such a major disaster, shown here near the Guadalupe area, was the beginning of Lubbock's pulling together in the crisis and rebuilding these areas to the benefit of the residents. From the Avalanche-Journal

In 1973, Texas Instruments opened its new plant, shown here under construction at the junction of University Avenue and Loop 289. It is the company's primary computer production facility. Courtesy of Lubbock Chamber of Commerce

Aerial photo of Lubbock, looking northwest, in 1972. The May 11, 1970, tornado passed diagonally from top left to middle right, behind the tall buildings, shattering windows and twisting the Great Plains building (tall building, center left) on its axis. The missing windows are visible in this photo. Several years ago, the building was restored as the Metro Tower and is in full use as an office building. The tall building on the right is the Lubbock National Bank. Directly across from it, the large white building is the present County Courthouse and behind it, to the right, the County Jail, to the left the old Post Office. Directly across from the new Courthouse is Court Place, an office building. The tall building directly in the center is the Federal Courthouse. The U-shaped red brick building, left center, is the old Lubbock Hotel, built in 1925. The tall building, far left, is the First National Pioneer Gas Building, which is faced largely with sheet glass and was hard hit during the tornado. Courtesy of Lubbock Chamber of Commerce

CHAPTER 4: 1950 - 1980

Dr. Lauro Cavazos, president of Texas Tech University and Health Sciences Center says of this institution, completed in 1973:
"The Medical School is only seven years old. Think what a remarkable achievement— to have created from essentially nothing, a medical school that has not only undergraduate students but also graduate programs and residency training programs. I consider this the most unique medical school in the United States. There are campuses in Amarillo, El Paso, Lubbock, and, we hope, in the future, one in the Permian Basin. Texas Tech Health Sciences Center and Medical School will serve patient care in 128,000 square miles, one-third of the state of Texas." Courtesy of Dr. Lauro Cavazos, Courtesy of Texas Tech Public Information Center

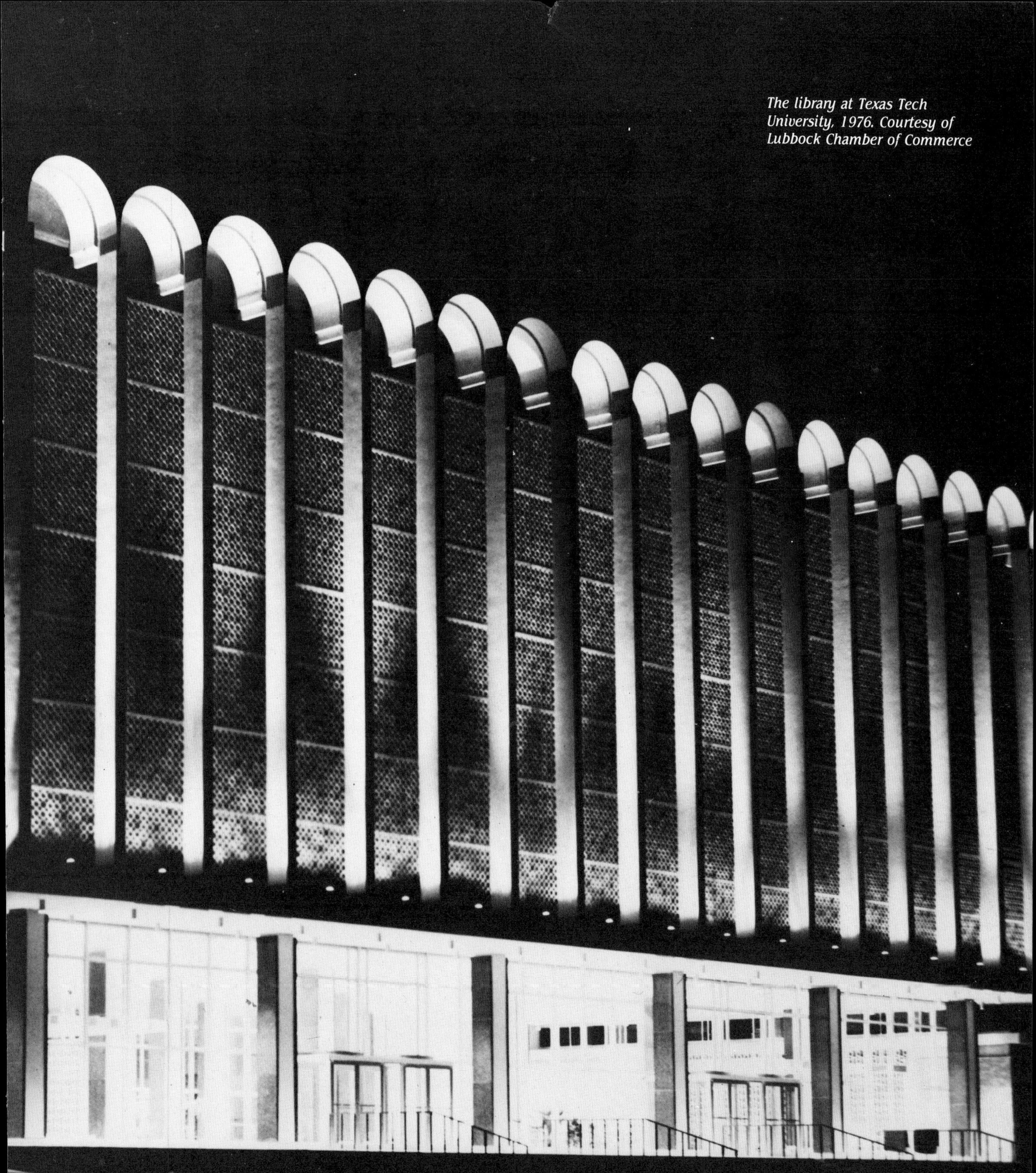

The library at Texas Tech University, 1976. Courtesy of Lubbock Chamber of Commerce

Ivy Green (Mrs. William T.) Savage was a long-respected educator in Lubbock. In addition to her almost twenty-five-year association with the Lubbock Public Schools, she served on many civic boards. During her forty-two-year career in education, she touched the lives of more than 10,000 students on the South Plains. While she was principal of Roscoe Wilson Elementary School, she compared today's students with those in her early teaching career: "They are all the same. Give them the right chance and they'll make good people." The Altrusa Club selected Mrs. Savage as Woman of the Year in 1964. She died November 10, 1976. Courtesy of Betty Savage Mills; courtesy of Avalanche-Journal

Congressman George Mahon with President Lyndon B. Johnson at the White House in the 1960s. Courtesy of Southwest Collection, Texas Tech University

The swimming pool in K. N. Clapp park, 1976. In 1931, a local civic leader, K. N. Clapp, leased the only pool in town, the Tumble-Inn, in Mackenzie Park when the city of Lubbock did not have the funds to operate it. Courtesy of Lubbock Chamber of Commerce

In this April 1972 photo, Congressman George Mahon is shown in his administrative office in Washington, D.C. He represented Lubbock and the district for forty-four distinguished years, from January 3, 1935, to May 1978.

The chandelier had been in the Oval Office in the White House when Franklin D. Roosevelt was president. Before the days of air conditioning, the windows were kept open during hot weather to catch whatever faint breezes might waft in. The tinkling of the crystal pendants annoyed Mr. Roosevelt, and he ordered the chandelier moved to this office.

Over the years, Mr. and Mrs. Mahon have welcomed thousands of visitors from the Lubbock area. They now live in Washington. Courtesy of Southwest Collection, Texas Tech University

Texas Boys Ranch is a unique area institution. In December 1972, a group of Christian men organized a home for dependent, neglected, and delinquent youth. Located on a ranch site five miles northeast of Lubbock, the ranch furnishes a cottage home environment, each for ten boys and the cottage parents.

Trained counselors from Tech and other agencies work with the boys on the ranch. Through involvement in ranch activities, boys learn social skills and regain self-esteem. Counselors also work with the boys and their families for their eventual return to their homes to become productive members of society.

Many a graduate of Texas Boys Ranch has gone on to help other boys who find themselves in desperate situations. Courtesy of Texas Boys Ranch

On July 4, 1976, in conjunction with the national bicentennial, Lubbock held a celebration. The parade down Broadway included an astonishing sight: a herd of Texas longhorn steers. Charles Schreiner III, of the YO Ranch, initiated the drive, which started from San Antonio and took several days, reminiscent of the old cattle drives. Courtesy of Lubbock Chamber of Commerce

A pony cart rides in the Centennial Parade, July 4, 1976. Courtesy of Lubbock Chamber of Commerce

One of Lubbock's early fire-fighting trucks—maybe the only one—from the 1920s rides in the Centennial Parade, July 4, 1976. Courtesy of Lubbock Chamber of Commerce

July 4, 1976: Boy Scouts proudly carry American flags, some from years past. Courtesy of Lubbock Chamber of Commerce

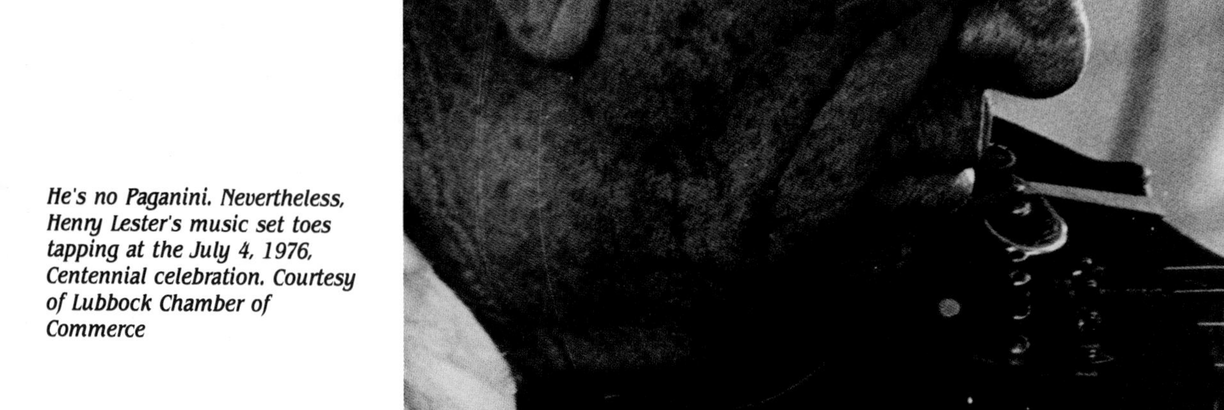

He's no Paganini. Nevertheless, Henry Lester's music set toes tapping at the July 4, 1976, Centennial celebration. Courtesy of Lubbock Chamber of Commerce

Willy Lusk, bootmaker to the famous, shown in 1971. He served a seven-year apprenticeship in San Angelo, to a Czechoslovakian bootmaker. Coming to Lubbock in 1934, he worked at a local boot and saddle shop. One day, a Las Vegas millionaire came in to pick up his custom-made Western boots, found the prices raised, and, with twenty-five $100 bills, staked Lusk to his own shop.

From all over the country, generals, movie stars, statesmen, and ordinary citizens flocked to Willy Lusk's shop. He contributed to Lubbock's economy in the tradition of the community—independent, industrious, one of the last of the vanishing breed of true artisans. He died July 3, 1976. Courtesy of Avalanche-Journal

Lubbock women have always been interested in handcrafts and have produced many beautiful items from the time of the first settlers until today. Here, Mrs. A. L. Henderson displays a quilt made by the Shakespeare Club for a firm in Wisconsin in 1978. Courtesy of Lubbock Chamber of Commerce

Water sports at Buffalo Lakes. Courtesy of City of Lubbock Public Information Office; courtesy of Lubbock Chamber of Commerce

Built in 1961 on the site of the old City Hall, this is the present City Hall. Courtesy of Lubbock Chamber of Commerce

WILLIAM CURRY HOLDEN
Teresita
HOLDEN
TERESITA
STEMMER HOUSE
A Yaqui Life

Dr. William Curry Holden, professor emeritus of history, Texas Tech University, is shown on September 22, 1980. The books are a part of his prolific literary output over the years as archeologist and historian. In 1923, he became head of the history department at McMurry College in Abilene, Texas. After leaving McMurry, he spent one year, 1927, at the University of Texas, then, in 1929, came to Tech as professor of history. In May 1929, he was chosen third vice-president of the newly formed Plains Museum Society, which held its first meeting February 30, 1930, with sixty-nine charter members. The entire collection consisted of "one branding iron, one cast iron 'son-of-a-gun' pot with a hole in the bottom, and one pack saddle for a burro, with all the leather gone." Holden was director of the Museum from 1929 until 1965.

One of the first to see the possibilities in the Lubbock Lake Site, a world-famous archeological "dig," Holden also established the Southwest Collection of archival materials. He was co-chairman of the Planning Commission for the Ranching Heritage Center, adjacent to the present Texas Tech Museum, and president of the Ranch Headquarters for 1970-72. Currently, he is a member of the committee for the National Golden Spur Award given annually to a person who has done outstanding work in the ranching and livestock industry. His wife, Fran, has been his enthusiastic partner in all their undertakings. From the Avalanche-Journal

Mackenzie State Park in winter. Built in the summer of 1935, originally as a Civilian Conservation Corps camp, the park was soon leased to the city of Lubbock by the state of Texas, a "unique situation as far as the operations of parks in the United States is concerned" (Graves, History of Lubbock*). Courtesy of Southwest Collection, Texas Tech University*

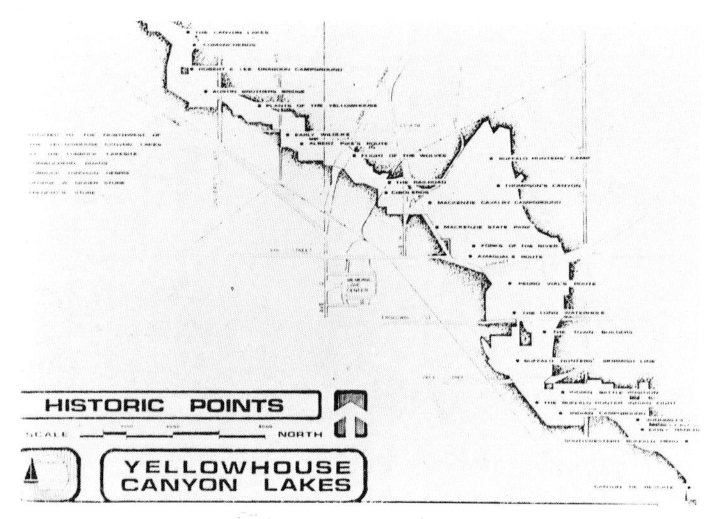

The Yellowhouse Canyon Lakes, 1980. Lubbock occupies a semi-arid section of the country, and water is all-important. The Yellowhouse Canyon draw meanders through Lubbock from northwest to southeast. It has been the site of Indian campgrounds, buffalo hunters' camps, military operations against the Indians, and, northwest, George W. Singer's store in 1890. In 1966, Lubbock initiated this water- and site-reclamation project. Existing parkland—Mackenzie State Park, Mae Simmons Park, and Helen Hodges Park—made a total of 653 acres. Additional land was acquired. From the nomadic hunters who used this canyon for water, hunting, and protection almost 20,000 years ago and the early Spanish explorers who saw the Indians' pueblo of yellow rock at the headwaters of the west fork of the Brazos and called the canyon "Casas Amarillos," or "Yellowhouses," to the present day, the canyon is an integral part of the annals of Lubbock and the Southwest. Courtesy of Lubbock Planning Department

Paleo-Indians existed on the South Plains in the Lubbock area 10,000-12,000 years ago. For the past several years, a sophisticated excavation has been going on at a point in Yellowhouse Draw just north and west of Lubbock at what archeologists call the Lubbock Lake Site. Folsom man left the first evidence of his hunts of the big bison and smaller game—arrowheads, scrapers, skinning and pounding tools. Explorers from all over the world have excavated heaps of discarded bones. Last summer, the expedition replicated Clovis-style butchering tools to test for function on a deceased circus elephant.

Here, in 1978, an explorer makes notes on his section of the digs. He takes care to ensure preservation of even the smallest artifact or relic.

The search continues. At least twenty feet more of lake-bottom sediment must be probed before paleo-Indian levels can be reached. Daily tours of the site are held during July and August. Courtesy of The Museum, Texas Tech University

Peter Hurd Mural

The South Plains Mural, a fresco by Peter Hurd, noted American artist and son-in-law of N. C. Wyeth, graces the walls of the 1,600 square-foot lobby of the former Museum on the Texas Tech campus. The building is now in use as Holden Hall, housing the department of art and design. It is named after Tech's Professor Emeritus of History, Dr. William Curry Holden, who, assisted by his wife, Fran, was the founder of the original Museum and of the Southwest Collection of archival records.

Comprised of sixteen panels measuring seventeen feet by thirty-nine feet, the mural was completed in October 1954 as a "permanent monument to those hardy pioneers who dared look at miles of barren plain and visualize churches, schools and homes amid vast areas of industry, farming, commerce and culture."

The Museum's board of directors appointed a Rotunda Selection Committee to choose individuals to be honored. Each of the people portrayed is recognized as a good neighbor who contributed his or her talents and skills to the development of the South Plains. Information courtesy of The Museum, Texas Tech University

Town builder Marion Virgil Brownfield (1854-1929), at left. Cowboy, trail driver, cattleman, colonizer, and banker, this public-spirited man helped found Brownfield, south of Lubbock.

Cowboy Sam C. Arnett (1876-1957), center, worked his first cattle at the age of six, later became a cattleman and banker. A rugged individualist and a judge of cattle, horses, and men, Arnett stayed through every drought and manmade crisis which came along.

Cattleman W. E. Halsell (1851-1934), at right. Left an orphan without funds, he became a cow hand, trail driver, and ranch foreman. With foresight and industry, he combined a number of ranches in Texas and Oklahoma.

Myriad details of South Plains life are featured in the background. The surveyor, the buggy, and the covered wagon stand on the main street of the early town. A sudden squall appears beyond the Eclipse windmill, the barbed wire fence, and the stock tank which holds scarce water. The ever-present mesquite is at far right. Courtesy of The Museum, Texas Tech University

Freighter Walter S. Posey (1881-1973) began freighting from Amarillo to Floydada, which is just east of Lubbock, at the age of eleven. At twenty-three, he became cashier of the First National Bank of Lubbock, an institution he was identified with for the rest of his life. He was accorded every civic honor Lubbock had to offer. Courtesy of The Museum, Texas Tech University

Civic leader Clifford B. Jones (1885-1972)—Businessman, ranchman, college president. From the appointment of the first board of directors in 1925, he was officially connected with Texas Tech until his retirement, when he became affiliated with a local bank. Courtesy of The Museum, Texas Tech University

Merchant Crone W. Furr (1878-1946), at left, established in 1904 the Kirland Mercantile Company, from which grew the Furr enterprises, now covering four states.

Lawyer William H. Bledsoe (1869-1936), center, arrived in Lubbock in 1908 and practiced law. He served two terms in the Texas House of Representatives. After election to the Senate, he wrote Senate Bill 103 creating Texas Technological College.

Circuit rider Robert Franklin Dunn (1855-1929), at right, whose circuit in 1881 included the cow camps and settlements from Amarillo to Sweetwater, a circuit which required three months travel on horseback. Devoted to the spiritual needs of the people of his area, he often held services from the back of a chuckwagon. Courtesy of The Museum, Texas Tech University

Banker Charles Earnest Maedgen (1882-1964), at left, arrived in Lubbock from Belton in 1917 and founded the forerunner of the Lubbock National Bank.

Journalist James Lorenzo Dow (1878-1958), center, acquired the Avalanche, *a five-column, four-page weekly, shortly after his 1908 arrival in Lubbock as a journeyman printer. In sixteen years, he had made it into a regional daily. He was a zealous editor who promoted civic causes with zeal but never failed to thunder his disapproval of any community flaw which, in his judgment, might harm Lubbock. Courtesy of The Museum, Texas Tech University*

Schoolteacher M. M. Dupre (1866-1925), at left, born in Ohio, came to Lubbock in 1914 to become a superintendent of schools. He was instrumental in organizing the Texas Interscholastic League, which still conducts statewide contests in various scholastic disciplines. He strongly advocated the establishment of a college in Lubbock, but died before he could see Texas Technological College open in 1925. He and his family lived in the 2000 block on Broadway.

Pioneer woman Dora Roberts, at right, was born in Alabama about 1876. She made several moves, ending in Coleman County. Married to a Mr. Griffin at the time, she skinned dead cattle and sold their hides to buy flour in order to combat their poverty. Through industry, she accumulated enough money to buy land. At the last, she owned hundreds of producing oil wells, but she never lost her habit of industry; she continued to raise chickens and take eggs into town in her Cadillac to sell. Courtesy of The Museum, Texas Tech University

Oilman Sid Richardson (1892-1959), at left, was a horsetrader, roustabout, and roughneck. In 1932, he leased, drilled, and completed fields in Ward and Winkler counties; in 1937, he did the same with the Slaughter field in Hockley County, south of Lubbock. Later, Richardson built oil processing plants. Starting his life without capital, in the best independent Texas tradition, he helped build West Texas and became a billionaire.

Doctor Marvin C. Overton (1878-1955), center, arrived in Lubbock from Louisville, Kentucky, in 1901, and found a smallpox epidemic. He practiced in a 125-mile radius in a horse and buggy, operating on kitchen tables by kerosene lamps under primitive conditions. He was a civic leader and an ardent supporter of his (Methodist) church. Everyday, he wore a fresh carnation in his buttonhole—his trademark.

The Chroniclers: Peter Hurd; J. Evetts Haley, cowboy-historian; William Curry Holden, archeologist-historian; Tom Lea, writer-artist; and John A. Lomax, collector of folk ballads, are preparing to bed down for the night in their bedrolls, after a dinner cooked over an open fire. Courtesy of The Museum, Texas Tech University

Dr. Clifford Jones (left) poses for Peter Hurd. Courtesy of The Museum, Texas Tech University

The new Museum at Texas Tech University at Fourth Street and Indiana Avenue, constructed 1970-76, covers seventy-six acres and encompasses a 160,000-square-foot main building and two outdoor exhibits, the Ranching Heritage Center and the Goodman Cotton Gin. The cone-shaped building at left is the Moody Planetarium, which can contain 100 people.

The Ranching Heritage Center, at upper left, outdoors, consists of thirty historic ranch structures that have been, at one time or another, moved to the twelve-acre site. A highly popular feature of the museum, the center attracts many visitors each year. The Ranching Center's buildings tell the fascinating story of the development of the livestock and ranching industry which was the foundation of this part of the American West. Do ghosts walk here at night?

Out of sight, at the right, is the Goodman cotton gin, a two-story structure built in 1875. It represents a transition between the old plantation gins and the early commercial gins.

In addition to these features, the museum contains classrooms, a library, work areas, and laboratories. On the main floor are exhibition galleries and a sales shop. Courtesy of The Museum, Texas Tech University

Aerial view of downtown Lubbock, 1976, showing, upper right, the newly constructed Memorial Civic Center. The tornado of May 11, 1970, had swept directly through this area on its way to the northeast, destroying everything in its path. Courtesy of Lubbock Chamber of Commerce

The Spur Granary, built in 1905, was used to store feed. The builder put the granary on a hill to save energy and time: Grain, shoveled into the granary's chutes, slid down to the grain boxes in the stalls at the base of the hill. Courtesy of The Museum, Texas Tech University

El Capote Cabin, built in about 1836, represents the turbulent era of the Republic of Texas. Courtesy of The Museum, Texas Tech University

The present-day Harrell House was built over a period of twenty-seven years, from 1883 to 1910. The house witnessed a large slice of the development of the Texas ranching industry. Courtesy of The Museum, Texas Tech University

The 1875 Joly Ranch Complex was built by a Palo Pinto County man who frequently left his family to work the cattle drives. The stone complex was the best he could do to protect his family in his absence. Courtesy of The Museum, Texas Tech University

The 1904 Picket and Sotol House— built of cedar posts and sotol stalks— was constructed as a temporary residence until a young ranching couple could afford to build a more comfortable dwelling. Courtesy of The Museum, Texas Tech University

Marjorie Meriwether Post Davies and her daughter, Dina Merrill Robertson, visit the Peter Hurd mural at the former Tech Museum.

Mrs. Davies' father, Charles W. Post, came to the South Plains about 1906 and purchased 150,000 acres of land to attract potential settlers (Graves, History of Lubbock*). This purchase changed the character of what had formerly been cattle land on the range to smaller sections of land which farmers purchased and started the emphasis on agriculture which remains the backbone of the Lubbock economy today. In the process, Post established the town of Post, several miles south of Lubbock.*

In addition to his larger undertakings, Post created that popular hot drink, Postum. He got the idea from the Plains natives, who boiled wheat and barley into a coffee-like drink which didn't jangle the drinker's nerves. Courtesy of Southwest Collection, Texas Tech University

Grain sorghum is one of the area's most lucrative crops. Along with cotton, alfalfa, and recently, sunflowers, this feed grain grows particularly well around Lubbock. As harvest nears, the heavy heads of grain present a thrilling sight. Courtesy of Lubbock Chamber of Commerce

In the summer of 1978, Roots Historical Arts Council, a group formed in 1977 to promote Black heritage on the Staked Plains, organized the group shown here. They re-enacted the sixty-five-mile expedition of the "Lost Battalion."

"In July, 101 years ago, Captain Nicholas Nolan and Company A, Tenth Cavalry, left Meadow in search of Indian raiders. The party baked in the murderous Texas sun for eighty-six hours without water. In desperation, the men drank the blood of their dying horses" in a desperate attempt to survive. Five men died (Lubbock Avalanche-Journal*). From the* Avalanche-Journal

Winner of the 1980 Adelita contest, Melissa Lynn Freeman dances with her partner, Jesus Montolvo. Adelita is chosen for her talent, costume, and knowledge of Mexican-American history during the annual four-day Fiestas Mexicanas. The Fiestas celebrate Mexican-Americans' pride in their national heritage and culminate in celebrating Diez y Seis de Septembre (the sixteenth of September), the date of Mexico's independence from Spain in 1821. Adelita was the Mexican heroine who helped win that independence. Risking her life to fight beside the soldiers, she engaged in battle, comforted the wounded, and lifted sagging spirits. She became so respected and admired that all other women who also joined their men in battle became known as "Adelitas."

The festival, which consists of religious ceremonies, dances, parades, and educational seminars, attracts people of all nationalities and helps illustrate the colorful heritage of the Mexican-Americans. From the Avalanche-Journal

"Weave 'em up 'n' weave 'em down, Weave them purty gals 'round 'n' 'round!"

Lubbock square dancers are hosts for a convocation of area dancers in 1978. Round and square dancing have been favorite forms of entertainment since the earliest days of Lubbock. Although the city has always been noted for being a strict religious community, paradoxically, dancing was an extremely popular form of entertainment. Dancing parties have always occurred frequently, sometimes with no excuse at all other than sheer enjoyment.

During the Depression years, says one Lubbock resident, "We used to go out to someone's farmhouse, take a hand-wound Victrola, wind it up and dance the night away— a cheap form of entertainment. We had a good time!" Courtesy of Lubbock Chamber of Commerce

In fall 1969, the Lubbock Theatre Center and the Lubbock Childrens' Theater needed dance features. As a result, the Lubbock Civic Ballet began presenting full-length dance programs. From then until 1980, several artistic directors served. Now, in the 1980-81 season, Leonid Lubarsky, graduate and principal of Leningrad's Kirov Ballet, is producing the ballet's third season of The Nutcracker Suite, *as well as a full-scale production of* Don Quixote. *In addition, in 1981, the ballet plans to present excerpts from its repertoire at the annual Lubbock Arts Festival before an estimated audience of 75,000.*

An April 6, 1980, production by the Lubbock Theatre Center of Moss Hart's and George M. Kaufman's You Can't Take It With You. *The Theatre Center has recently occupied the old Lindsey Theatre at the corner of Main Street and Avenue J. The original Lindsey Theatre was built on Main Street in 1916 by Jefferson Davis Lindsey. In the late 1930s, the building was replaced with the present structure. In 1940, the new Lindsey opened its doors with the movie* The Mark of Zorro, *starring Tyrone Power.*

The Lubbock Theatre Center is a community theatre and provides an outlet for people interested in amateur theatre. LTC also sponsors a children's theatre and theatre school to encourage children in the performing arts.

Clockwise, from far left: Tom Curtis, Tony Mitchell, Gary Walters, Rebecca Rugel, Sylvia Ashby, Sarah Einerson, Cindy Chaney, Bill Conley, Jane Prince Jones, Steve Nelson, and Kevin Howard. Courtesy of Lubbock Theatre Center

Kent Hance, center, United States Representative since January 1978 from the nineteenth Congressional district of Texas (encompassing Reese Air Force Base), talks with Reese personnel during a mission orientation visit to the base in 1979.

Congressman Hance assesses Lubbock's character: "The city and surrounding communities, their people and their way of life are to be cherished. We have good people, active churches, a strong economy, fertile soils, clear skies, and magnificent sunsets.

"The spirit of the nation, that old-fashioned patriotism around which the country was built, does not need to be rekindled in Lubbock— here it was never lost. Lubbock pioneers, like our leaders today, did not give up through fear, indifference, or apathy. This is our heritage and tradition. We shall maintain it." Courtesy of Reese Air Force Base Office of Public Information

In 1957, Mac Davis was a Lubbock High School sophomore. By this time, he was entertaining classmates with his guitar and songs. His latest hit, in 1980, "Lubbock, Texas in My Rear View Mirror," ends, "You can bury me in Lubbock in my jeans." Courtesy of Casablanca Records and Filmworks Co., Inc., manufacturers and distributors

In 1947, Mac Davis, age five (far left, second row), accompanied his six-year-old sister, Linda Kay, to Mrs. Jackson's Private School at 2410 Sixteenth Street. Mrs. Mattie M. Jackson stands at top left. The house still stands. Later, Mac skipped two grades and was graduated from Lubbock High School at sixteen, in 1958. After graduation, he enrolled at Emory University, Atlanta, Georgia, for two years. From there, after a stint writing releases for a recording company, he became a top song writer and entertainer. Courtesy of T. J. Davis

Ernest Martinez, shown here on July 4, 1980, starts his Model A Ford with the original lug crank. In 1954, he paid a Texas Tech student $450 for the canary yellow Ford with a rumble seat and an ah-oo-gah horn. His sons used it as a hot rod during their school years. When he retired, Martinez became bored. To keep busy and to recoup some of the expense of restoring the car, he painted it Washington blue and turned it into a taxi. The car draws a lot of attention in Lubbock as it chugs efficiently along at twenty-eight miles to the gallon! From the Avalanche-Journal

Black gold! During Lubbock's booming 1940s, petroleum exploration and production became equally important to the Lubbock area as cotton. Courtesy of Orville Stevenson

White diamonds! As early as 1896, the first cotton came to Lubbock, and by 1900, cotton was an established significant crop. Over the years, come drought or plentiful rainfall, cotton continues to be the backbone of the area's economy. Courtesy of Avalanche-Journal

A typical West Texas pioneer family is portrayed on this statue commissioned by the American State Bank in 1971. These sturdy forebears of present-day Lubbock citizens carry the tools from which the community was forged: his hoe, her Bible and the flower she carries, and the future cattleman's lariat. The bronze stands in a small park next to the bank at Thirteenth Street and Avenue Q. Courtesy of Granville Carter, sculptor, and the American State Bank

Bibliography

In 1891, when the Caraway farm was built at what is now the junction of Indiana Avenue and Fiftieth Street, at Winchester Square, Lubbock was four miles away. The Eclipse windmill, with wooden blades, was built the same year. Fiftieth Street was a cowtrail bordered with mulberry trees. About 1925, metal blades replaced the wooden ones. Monterey High School football field stands on the site of what was then an orchard of apple, pear, plum, cherry, peach, and walnut trees. Antelope came right up to the Caraway farm and provided a source of food on many occasions, and the windmill furnished neighbors for miles around with water. A mulberry tree still stands next to the Eclipse windmill. Courtesy of Lubbock Chamber of Commerce

Andrews, Ruth Horn. *The First Thirty Years of Tech.* Lubbock: Texas Tech Press, 1956.

Connor, Seymour V., ed. *Builders of the Southwest.* Lubbock: Southwest Collection, Texas Technical College,1959.

Evans, Wanda. *One Honest Man.* Canyon, Texas: Staked Plains Press, 1976.

Ford, Gus. *Texas Cattle Brands.* 2nd ed. Dallas: Clyde Cockrell, 1958.

Graves, Lawrence L., ed. *A History of Lubbock.* Lubbock: West Texas Museum Association, Texas Technical College, 1962.

Griggs, William, et al., ed. *A Pictorial History of Lubbock, 1880-1950.* Lubbock County Historical Commission, 1976.

Johnson, Virginia M. *The Unregimented General: A Biography of Nelson A. Miles.* Boston: Houghton Mifflin, 1962.

The Llano Estacado. Norman: University of Oklahoma Press, 1953.

The *Lubbock Avalanche-Journal.* Morris Publishing.

Lynch, Etta. *Tender Tyrant.* Canyon, Texas: Staked Plains Press, 1976.

Tijerina, Andres A. *A History of the Mexican Americans in Lubbock County.* M.A. thesis, Texas Tech University, 1973.

Weems, John Edward. *Death Song: The Last of the Indian Wars.* Garden City, N.Y.: Doubleday, 1976.

Index